Setting Up the Supply Network in SAP APO

Shaun Snapp

Setting Up the Supply Network in SAP APO

For information about this title or to order other books and/or electronic media, contact the publisher:
SCM Focus Press
PO Box 29502 #9059
Las Vegas, NV 89126-9502
http://www.scmfocus.com/scmfocuspress
(408) 657-0249

ISBN: 978-1-939731-09-8
Printed in the United States of America
Cover and interior design by: 1106 Design

Contents

CHAPTER 1

Introduction to the Supply Network

All of the books at SCM Focus Press focus on topics that are poorly addressed in the industry or have been addressed in a limited manner in other books; this criterion must be met before performing research and writing a book. Secondly, the author of any SCM Focus Press book has to have actually worked in, analyzed, configured, and tested the software of the specific topic areas. Thus, the reader can be assured that all the bases are covered and that the content is based upon real project experience.

Having read all of the books on SAP APO, I can say with confidence that this book is unique. It is the only book on supply planning to focus entirely on how to set up supply networks in APO and how to meet highly-customized requirements that relate to network design—topics that are not covered in SAP training classes in any depth. When taking an SAP training class (from SAP at least) the master data for the supply network is normally already set up, and the focus of the class is on planning the movements through the supply-planning network. Because of this, there is little time spent explaining how to set up APO.

My previous book, *Supply Planning with MRP, DRP and APS Software,* can be seen as a companion to this book (at least for people interested in APO), as it covers methods of supply planning only. In it, I combined coverage of the different supply planning methods with advice about—and historical analysis of—improving supply-planning implementations. I also provided information about optimization in general, both outside and inside of APO.

However, this book, which can be considered an advanced book, covers only the topic of how to set up the SNP model. APO requires a lot of set up to work properly. Of all the applications I have worked with, APO (regardless of the module) takes more effort to set up than other competing applications and this applies to any module in the suite. And that is just to set up the APO for the standard flows. The most complicated or sophisticated parts of the book deal with the non-standard workflows, for instance, where a location must be planned which is not an actual internal location to the supply network. Many business requirements necessitate a nonstandard network design and flow which impacts everything from the physical master data set-up, to the parameters used, to the sequence of planning runs and problem division, to what billing documents are created and when. So while this book will not be an easy read, I have expended considerable effort making the topics as easy to understand as possible. If I had come across this book several years ago, it would have answered many of my questions and increased considerably my ability to add value in my consulting work.

Another important thing to consider is that there are often several different ways of meeting the requirements for nonstandard supply planning designs. Each is typically a series of trade-offs. In meetings I often hear people make very black and white statements about requirements that need a design solution. For example, the business will state that certain requirements are "must haves," while IT will say that the same requirement is "not valid." I generally don't agree with either of these statements. As a consultant, it's not my job (and it is certainly not the job of IT) to determine whether a business requirement is valid. On the other hand, the amount of effort to maintain some solutions can make them poor implementation choices. In many cases the decision simply comes down to the resources that the company is willing to dedicate to the solution; the solution must match the short-term and long-term resources that the company is willing to dedicate. While some alternatives may be easier for planners to use, they may impose high long-term maintenance costs on the company.

I encourage those attempting to find the best solution to take the time to evaluate several solutions thoroughly before making a selection. It takes a while for the brain to process all of the different alternatives, and the first solution is often not the best. Pride of authorship can also be a barrier to evaluating choices, as the authors of one alternative may be biased toward their own solution. And even if the decision ends up being incorrect, I have noticed that companies tend to unite around the solution, and are very hesitant to change it. So I try to keep an open mind until all the facts are on the table. When I consult, I do not go into a company with the intention of implementing the same solution that I have implemented at another company. Slight adjustments are usually required for a new environment, and sometimes a whole different approach is best.

Reality-based Writing
The vast majority of material available on SAP has a positive bias, with writers presenting the official story (the happy path) of how SAP functionality works. Almost all of the authors who write about SAP work for consulting companies or for SAP itself; therefore, their freedom to write accurately about the good, bad and the ugly of SAP is essentially nonexistent. Throughout this book I present not only how APO is designed to work, but also how I have seen it work (and

not work) in practice. APO is now a widely implemented product (especially the more popular modules like DP, SNP, PP/DS and GATP) and there are some areas of functionality that work well and some that continue to be problematic. Sometimes these issues are related to areas that are simply nonfunctional, but they can also be related to areas that "work" but for which the maintenance costs are so high that they are unlikely to be sustained with the funding large companies tend to allocate to their supply chain planning function. Many executive decision makers, constantly in search of ways to justify previous decisions, continually take the approach of hoping that the next release will solve whatever problems APO has; however, this is not a strategy that I have seen work. If companies and consultants obtained better information about good and bad functionality, they could make better decisions, save a lot of money, and experience better solutions and outcomes.

Virtual Locations

In addition to covering the umbrella topic of supply planning networks, I discuss several niche areas such as virtual locations. There is very little material available on these topics, either in book form or on SAP Help, and the material that does exist is not nearly as helpful as it could be in providing instruction about setting up the system. In fact, there is little information on these topics outside of SAP Help. Therefore, this book should be useful to those looking for information on setting up a supply-planning network in SAP and non-SAP systems, as well as those looking for specifics on the niche topics I have mentioned.

The Use of Screen Shots in the Book

I consult in some popular and well-known applications, and I've found that companies have often been given the wrong impression of an application's capabilities. As part of my consulting work, I am required to present the results of testing and research about various applications. The research may show that a well-known application is not able to perform some functionality well enough to be used by a company, and point to a lesser-known application where this functionality is easily performed. Because I am routinely in this situation, I am asked to provide evidence of the testing results within applications, and screen shots provide this necessary evidence.

Furthermore, some time ago it became a habit for me to include extensive screen shots in most of my project documentation. A screen shot does not, of course, guarantee that a particular functionality works, but it is the best that can be done in a document format. Everything in this book exists in one application or another, and nothing described in this book is hypothetical.

Disclaimer on the Field Definitions

This book in parts has a large number of field definitions. As with my book, *Planning Horizons, Calendars and Timings in APO* (which had an enormous number of field definitions), I needed some portions of the SAP Help definitions, I did not want to use all of SAP's definition, and I also wanted to be able to weave in my take on the definition but without making the reader continually stop and start (between SAP's definition and my definition). Therefore, I settled on using the portions of the field definitions from SAP, but in combination with my shorthand. Some of the definitions are quite lengthy, so I have tried to provide a synopsis of them, and add some translation where necessary. I did not want to be concerned with separating out the exact SAP quotations from my text, so I am putting this disclaimer at the beginning of this book. *I am not trying to take credit for SAP's work, or say that any of the field definitions in this book are original*. I could have included the full definition of each field in this book, but that would have made the book quite tedious. That is why I think providing a synopsis is more valuable to readers. The definitions are the starting point; I have a layer of analysis and learning aids like graphics that help clarify many of the time settings. Finally, I have not included every timing field in every category. I have covered most of them, but some are very infrequently used.

How Writing Bias is Controlled at SCM Focus and SCM Focus Press

Bias is a serious problem in the enterprise software field. Large vendors receive uncritical coverage of their products, and large consulting companies recommend the large vendors that have the resources to hire and pay consultants rather than the vendors with the best software for the client's needs.

Just as in my consulting practice, I do not financially benefit from a company's decision to buy an application that I showcase in print, either in a book or on the website. SCM Focus has the most stringent rules related to controlling bias and restricting commercial influence of any information provider. These "writing rules" are provided in the link below:

http://www.scmfocus.com/writing-rules/

If other information providers followed these rules, I would be able to learn about software without being required to perform my own research and testing for every topic.

Information about enterprise supply chain planning software can be found on the Internet, but this information is primarily promotional or written at such a high level that none of the important details or limitations of the application are exposed; this is true of books as well. When only one enterprise software application is covered in a book, one will find that the application works perfectly; the application operates as expected and there are no problems during the implementation to bring the application live. This is all quite amazing and quite different from my experience of implementing enterprise software. However, it is very difficult to make a living by providing objective information about enterprise supply chain software, especially as it means being critical at some point. I once remarked to a friend that SCM Focus had very little competition in providing untarnished information on this software category, and he said, "Of course, there is no money in it."

The Approach to the Book

By writing this book, I wanted to help people get exactly the information they need without having to read a lengthy volume. The approach to the book is essentially the same as to my previous books, and in writing this book I followed the same principles.

1. **Be direct and concise.** There is very little theory in this book and the math that I cover is simple. This book is focused on software and for most users and implementers of the software the most important thing to understand is conceptually what the software is doing.

2. **Based on project experience.** Nothing in the book is hypothetical; I have worked with it or tested it on an actual project. My project experience has led to my understanding a number of things that are not covered in typical supply planning books. In this book, I pass on this understanding to you.

3. **Saturate the book with graphics.** Roughly two-thirds of a human's sensory input is visual, and books that do not use graphics—especially educational and training books such as this one—can fall short of their purpose. Graphics have also been used consistently and extensively on the SCM Focus website.

Before writing this book, I spent some time reviewing what has already been published on the subject. This book is different from other books in terms of its intended audience and its scope. It is directed toward people that have either worked with ERP or know what it is; I am assuming that the reader has a basic knowledge level in this area.

The SCM Focus Site

As I am also the author of the SCM Focus site, http://www.scmfocus.com, the site and the book share a number of concepts and graphics. Furthermore, this book contains many links to articles on the site, which provide more detail on specific subjects. This book provides an explanation of how supply and production planning software works and aims to continue to be a reference after its initial reading. However, if your interest in supply planning software continues to grow, the SCM Focus site is a good resource to which articles are continually added.

The SCM site dedicated specifically to supply planning is

   http://www.scmfocus.com/supplyplanning

The site dedicated to SAP planning is

   http://www.scmfocus.com/sapplanning

Intended Audience

The feedback I received from early reviewers described this book as good for any person who wants to understand how to set up SNP and all the related issues that surround this topic. If you have any questions or comments on the book, please email me at shaunsnapp@scmfocus.com.

Abbreviations

A listing of all abbreviations used throughout the book is provided at the end of the book.

CHAPTER 2

Locations in APO

We will discuss the different types of locations that can be set up in
SAP APO. In addition we will look at some creative setups that can
be employed to model supply planning networks to meet requirements. However, in order to understand these topics, it is necessary
to understand that in SAP APO, a location is a master data object
that that will manage material. Locations in APO have the following attributes:

1. Material can be produced and stored in locations.

2. Once a location is created, it can be viewed using either the
   Planning Book or the Product View, which are two of the main
   user interface transactions in APO. Screen shots are provided
   in this book. Any type of location used in APO can be shown in
   the user interface transactions, not just true physical locations.
   Inside of these views or user interfaces, SNP applies standardized rules as to how the material flows between the locations and
   between the key figures in the Planning Book, and the values in
   the Product View. (A good overview is provided in this article:

http://www.scmfocus.com/sapplanning/2012/10/15/understanding-the-flow-of-strs-and-prs-through-apo-with-a-custom-deployment-solution/)[1]

3. Every location in APO must be set up in the Location Master, which contains all the pertinent data regarding the location. A Product Master performs the same function for each product; a Product Location Master combines attributes from the product and location into one master data object.

Below I list some of the most important location tabs. APO has a Location Master, a Product Master and a Product Location Master. The Product Location Master is a combination of the Location and the Product Master; some of the master data settings are assigned to a location, some are assigned to the product, and others apply only at the intersection of product and location. When I cover master data in most of my other books, I talk about the Product Location Master. However, this book will be different. I don't focus on the Product Master or the Product Location Master, as they are not relevant for supply network design. Instead I will discuss the fields in the Location Master. One example of this is shown in the following screen shot:

---

[1] This book is focused on supply planning design, and is less focused on the methods used in supply planning, or the flow of material between locations. For these topics see my other books, *Supply Planning with MRP, DRP and APS Software,* and *Multi-method Supply Planning in SAP APO*—respectively.

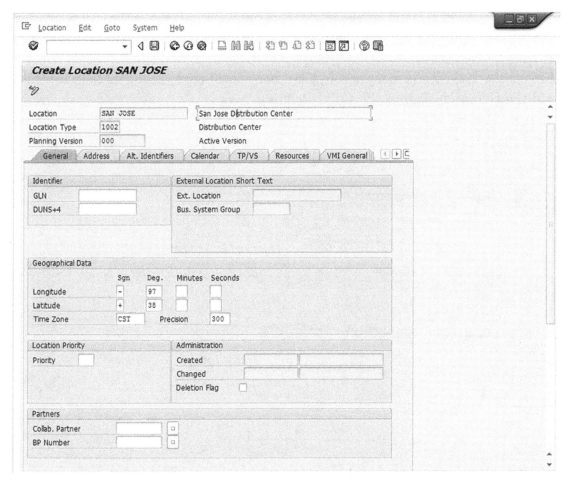

This location contains the geographic data about the location. (However, for locations that are actually connected by a transportation lane, the durations in the transportation lanes control how long it takes to move between locations.) There is also a location priority field, which allows the location to be assigned a certain priority in the overall supply network. These priorities have the following implications for the following areas of APO.

The Location Priority

Locations can be assigned a priority that controls the sequence in which they are processed. The priority could be used if some locations have a higher service level target than others. If some locations are processed before others, and there is a limited amount of stock to go around, then of course the locations processed earlier will have more of their demands met than those that are processed later.

The location priority only works with the Capable to Match (CTM) supply planning method and the TP/VS module that I discuss briefly in a few paragraphs.

The location priority is assigned in the Location Master, and this field interacts with the Demands Tab in the CTM Profile.

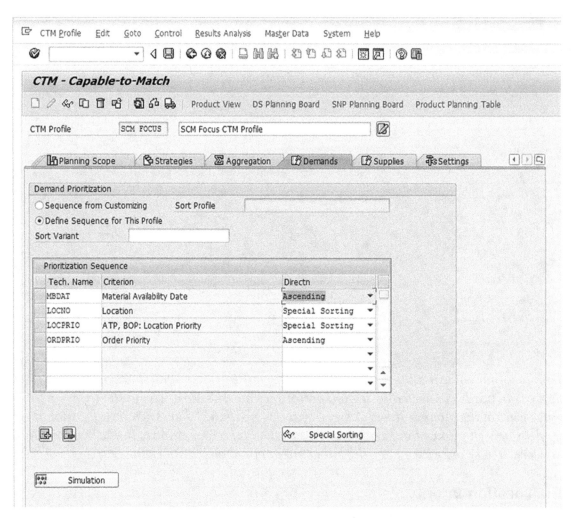

The location priority: I have added two location priorities (one for normal and demand and one for backorder processing) in the CTM Profile above, as a normal prioritization sequence. The higher the location is placed in the priority sequence, the more powerful its control over how CTM sequences its planning run.

Transportation Planning and Vehicle Scheduling (TP/VS)
TP/VS uses this location priority for its cost profile. Orders for locations where the destination location has the relevant priority are assigned the associated penalty costs for earliness, lateness or non-delivery. However, I don't cover TP/VS in this book, so I will not get into this functionality except to note that SNP is not the only module in APO to use the location priority field on the Location Master.

How the Location Priority Works
Enter the value "1" for the highest priority. The higher the number entered, the lower the priority. If you do not enter a value, the system automatically assigns the value "0," giving the location the highest priority.

Focus On   The Location Priority

Location-related priority is a complex topic in SAP APO. For this reason I include this *Focus On* section before leaving the topic and moving on to the rest of the Location Master tabs. While I focus on SNP throughout most of this book, I need to give a full account of the topic by covering how all of the modules use location prioritization. When I reviewed the various articles I had written on prioritization over the years at SCM Focus, I noticed that I did not give an integrated view of how location priority works throughout the APO suite (this occurs when one researches one application or setting only to fill a particular project need). However, with this book, I have finally produced the integrated view that I think many are looking for.

Different Location Fields and Functionality
To keep the various priorities straight, I have created the following matrix:

SNP Priorities

	Field Name	Located Where?	The Focus of the Field	Works with Which Modules?	Works with Which Supply Planning
Within the Location	Location Priority	Location Master	Location Sequence Processing	CTM, TP/VS	Initial Supply Plan
	Product Priority	Product Location Master	Used to Sequence Planned Orders -- in PP/DS, Deployment Optimizer and Capacity Leveling	SNP, PP/DS	Initial Supply Plan (Capacity Leveling), Deployment
	PPM/PDS Priority	On the PPM or PDS	Controls Which PPM or PDS is Used First	SNP, PP/DS	Initial Supply Plan
On the Transp.Lane	Distribution Priority	Product Specific Transportation Lane	Product Flow	SNP	Deployment
	Procurement Priority	Product Specific Transportation Lane	Product Flow for PP/DS, Location Sequence Processing for SNP	SNP, PP/DS	Deployment

This matrix compares and contrasts the various priorities. Notice that the priorities have different applications in different modules in SAP APO.

- *Location Priority:* This field is on the General Tab of the Product Location Master. The field controls the sequence of processing of the location or is used by TP/VS (as I have stated previously, I will not focus on TP/VS as it is a very specialized and infrequently-implemented module within APO). Location Priority is used for CTM when the demand category LOCPRIO— ATP, BOP: Confirmed Portion (Back Order Processing) is added to the order selection. This is shown in the following screen shot:

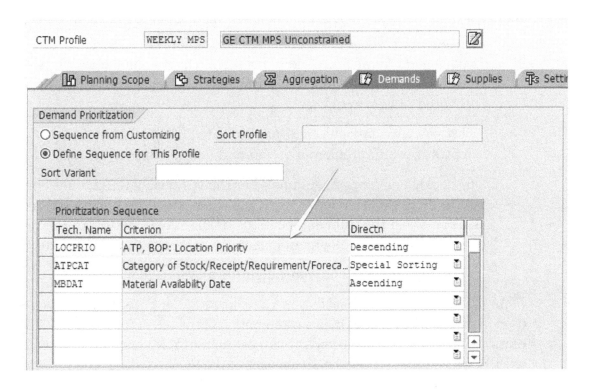

- *Product Priority:* On the SNP 2 tab of the Product Location Master. Product Priority is related to the following areas of functionality:

- *Capacity Leveling:* Whether to capacity-level based upon the product priority is defined in the SNP capacity-leveling profile. This field is called "Order Prioritization." I won't go into this topic here because I cover it in the book, *Constrained Supply and Production Planning in SAP APO.*
  - *PP/DS Order Sequence:* It controls the order by which material is scheduled in PP/DS. Thus, the priority helps to sequence the production orders for all production orders for a specific date and for a specific production line (priority can only be used to sort among products to be applied to similar resources). If the scheduling heuristic SAP001 is used, products with a higher priority will be scheduled before products with a lower priority (this would only matter if both

products share the same PPM/PDS). This heuristic is called (logically enough) "schedule sequence based upon the priority."[2]

- ○ *Deployment Optimizer:* Used to prioritize the decomposition or problem division of the deployment problem. The topic of decomposition is covered in this article:

  http://www.scmfocus.com/sapplanning/2011/10/12/snp-optimizer-sub-problem-division-and-decomposition/

  The deployment optimizer runs after the network optimizer has been run and creates the deployment plan: the stock transport requisitions between the internal locations in the supply network. A series of articles on the deployment optimizer can be found at this link:

  http://www.scmfocus.com/sapplanning/tag/deployment/.[3]

- • *PPM/PDS Priority:* This priority controls which PPM or PDS for production is used first. The PPM and PDS is a combination of the bill of materials (BOM), routing and resource. So a company can set up multiple versions of the PPM or PDS, which differ across the dimensions of the BOM, routing, and resource (or all three), and then set the preferred PPM/PDS. When the capacity or the material of the primary PPM/PDS is consumed, SNP will automatically move to the next PPM/PDS in the priority sequence. (More on the PPM/PDS

---

[2] Overall, I am not sold on using the production planning and scheduling system to determine the production priority of products. To me, this is the natural role of the supply planning system at least within the context of APO. In my view, the priorities should have been taken care of before the planned orders arrive at the production location. However, for the vendor PlanetTogether, whose design first performs the production plan and schedule and then creates the supply plan, this would be a logical approach. I cover supply planning first versus production planning first designs in the book, *The Superplant Concept.*

[3] Because the deployment optimizer naturally prioritizes the order type, it will prioritize sales orders above forecasts. However, this should not be confused with the Product Master priority, which I discuss in this section. The Product Master is only used as described above to decompose the problem so that the products with the higher priority are processed first.

at these articles: http://www.scmfocus.com/sapplanning/2012/07/27/
the-connection-between-boms-routings-work-centers-in-erp-and-ppms-pdss-
in-apo/).[4]

The PPM/PDS priority does not help SNP make decisions between locations; it helps SNP choose the best PPM/PDS among a series of alternatives
within a location. The functionality to make decisions between locations
that can all produce the same product is called multi-plant planning. This
functionality is not available within SNP. More on this topic can be found
at the following link:

> http://www.scmfocus.com/productionplanningandscheduling/
> 2013/04/22/multi-plant-planning-definition/

- *The (Transportation Lane) Distribution Priority:* This priority is on the
  Product Specific Transportation Lane. This is discussed in Chapter 3:
  "Transportation Lanes" and is related to distributing stock during
  deployment.

- *Procurement Priority:* This is also on the Product Specific Transportation
  Lane and is covered in Chapter 3: "Transportation Lanes." This is used
  both for deployment and for source determination (that is for both the initial supply plan and for deployment). How it is used greatly depends upon
  both the module and in the case of SNP, the method within the module.
  - It is used by PP/DS for source determination.
  - It is used by SNP deployment to determine the sequence of process-
    ing for deployment. The priority applies to the destination location
    of the transportation lane.

---

[4] One might ask how switching to a different PPM/PDS based upon a material constraint would make
any difference. It's a good question. However, identical finished goods can have different input materials
as part of its BOM (remember a different BOM means a different PPM/PDS), but different machinery
can also mean a different consumption level of material. Some machines (resources) are inherently more
efficient and waste fewer products than others. Therefore, one PPM/PDS could be material constrained
in meeting demand, whereas another PPM/PDS may not. This is part of the larger issue of the alternate
PPM/PDS varying among any dimension of BOM, resource or routing.

- ○ It is used for the SNP optimizer if automatic cost generation is enabled (which is in fact quite rare—I have yet to see it used at a client). Enabled by the Procurement Priority of the PPM/PDS or Procurement Priority of Transportation Lanes in the SNP Deployment Profile. This is shown in the screen shot below:

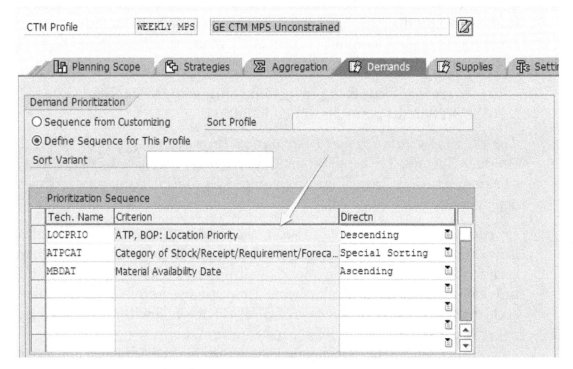

Here is the Demand Tab in the CTM Profile. If the LOCPRIO—ATP, BOP: Confirmed Portion (Back Order Processing) is at the top of the sequence—as I have shown it in the screen shot above, then CTM will process demands first in a location sequence. A company may choose to prioritize customers within this sequence or not. In this demand sequence I have defined above, the location controls the first sequence of demand as it flows through CTM and material availability date is sorted last. All of these things come down to how a

company wants to allocate a limited supply. The more limited the supply, the more control the various sort sequences have over the supply plan and who will get the limited stock.

SNP actually has a number of other prioritization capabilities, including the following:

1. PPM/PDS Prioritization: Used to create primary and secondary combinations of routings, BOMs and resources.

2. Transportation Lane Prioritization: Used to control the flow of product through the network by giving some transportation lanes priority over others.

3. Product Prioritization: Used when some products have a higher service level target than others. It will direct the supply network resources to be allocated to delivering some products over others.

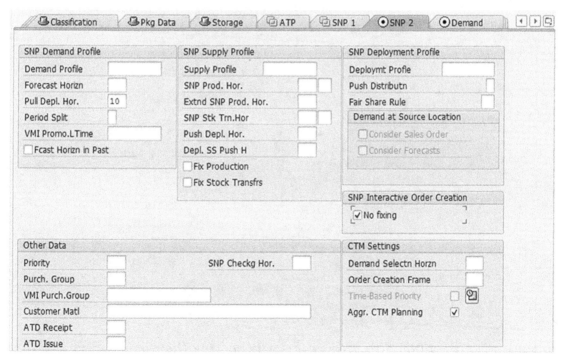

The product location priority is used differently from the location priority. First, it is used for PP/DS while the location priority is not.

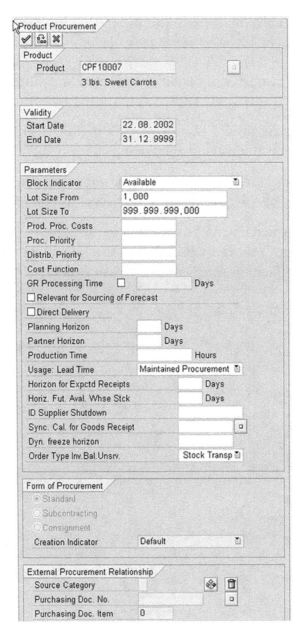

Here we can see both the Procurement Priority and the Distribution Priority Fields. This can be applied for all products or for different products, meaning that some products could have a priority between locations, and other products could have a different priority or no priority. As a side note, all priorities are subordinate to the existence of a

quota arrangement. If a quota arrangement is in effect for a transportation lane, then the quota arrangement is used by SNP (quota arrangements are percentage based). This is true regardless of whether there is a priority on the transportation lane. A priority is only used to control flow if no quota arrangement is applied.

Location Prioritization and Multi-sourcing

Prioritization of locations leads directly into the topic of multi-sourcing. Multi-sourcing is the ability for a supply planning system to intelligently choose between alternate sources of supply. For instance, if a company has several supply sources, then a supply planning system that could automatically select the best option would be a significant advantage for that company.

Here is one common scenario for multi-sourcing. When the primary location cannot handle the capacity of the order, the supply planning system would move to a second or even third location in order to satisfy the demand. Another reason for multi-sourcing can be to spread, by rough percentages, the total demand among various sources of supply. Multi-sourcing is a common requirement that drives companies to use the SNP Optimizer. Multi-sourcing is covered in more detail in Chapter 4: "Sources of Supply and Multi-sourcing."

SNP changes the priority that it uses based upon whether the product is produced internally or purchased externally. Without the optimizer, and just based upon priorities, SNP cannot use both the priority on the PPM/PDS and the priority on the transportation lane. Instead it uses one or the other. SAP has the following to say about the topic:

> *If you have specified the In-House Production procurement type in the location product master, the system considers the procurement priority in the PPM or in the PDS. **If you have specified External Procurement as the procurement type, the system considers the procurement priority in the transportation lane**. With procurement type In-House Production or External Procurement, the system compares the procurement priority from the transportation lane with the procurement priority in the PPM or PDS. The source of supply with the lower value for the procurement priority has priority over the source*

of supply with the higher value. The highest procurement priority is the value zero. —SAP Help

More Location Tabs in the Location Master

The following tabs are available on the Location Master in APO:

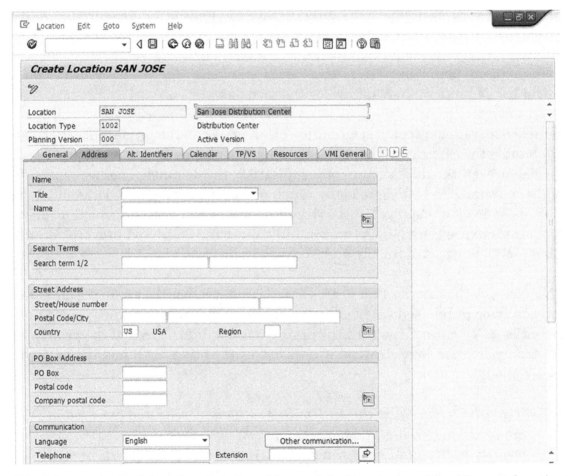

All of the particularities related to the address of the location are listed here. A location, such as a shipping point, will have the same address as its parent location—or the location that it is housed within.

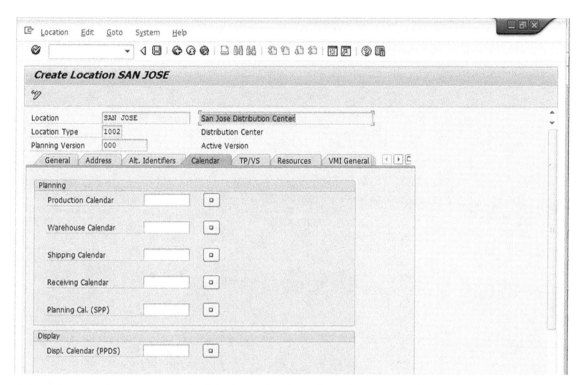

A location can be associated with the calendars listed above. Calendars control when the location can perform the activities specific to each calendar. If a location is associated with a calendar that has only five hours per day available for shipping, five days a week, then that is the window—or the capacity—that the location will have for shipping. Each location can be associated with only one calendar type at a time (that is one production calendar); however, calendars can be easily changed for large numbers of locations with the MASSD transaction. Also, calendars can be assigned flexibly so that each location can have one calendar, or can have a customized calendar per location. There is a tendency to think of resources as one of the only types of constraints. However, a calendar is just as much a constraint as a resource. A resource has a particular capacity; however, that capacity is only available within the calendar that is assigned to the location. For extensive details on calendars see the book, Planning Horizons, Calendars and Timing in SAP APO.

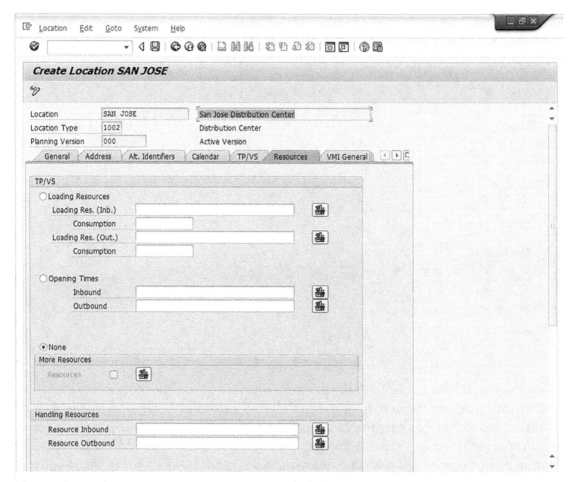

These are all of the resources that can be assigned to the location. Notice that this is a distribution center location type, (there is a storage resource entry field further down on this screen). However, there is no entry field for a production resource.

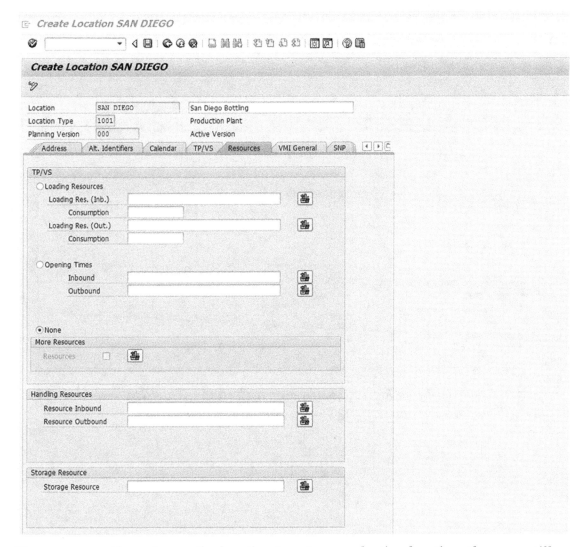

However, even if we change the location type to a production location, there are still no entry fields for production resources. This is because resources are not assigned to a location in the Location Master. Instead they are assigned to the PPM/PDS. Notice this from the screen shot on the following page:

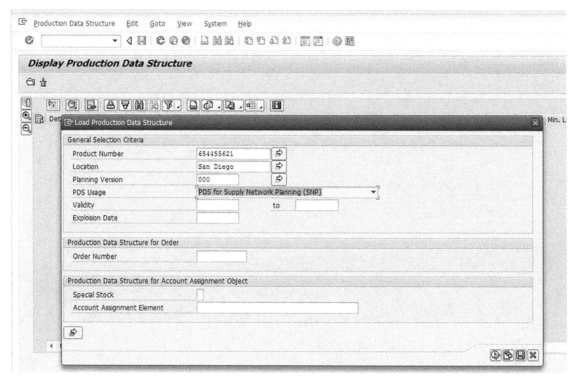

Notice that when searching for a PDS, we state its location. The PDS and the PPM are assigned to the location and of course to the planning version.

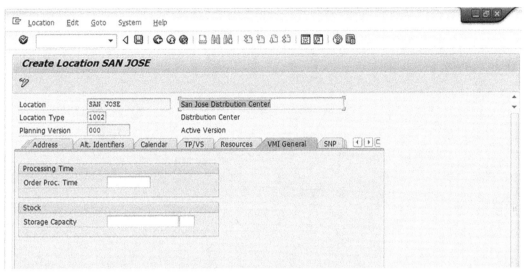

This is a vendor-managed inventory location and includes fields for the order processing time and the storage capacity of the location. Storage capacity is not used for SNP, but instead for SNC (Supplier Network Collaboration), which is not a module that I cover in this book.

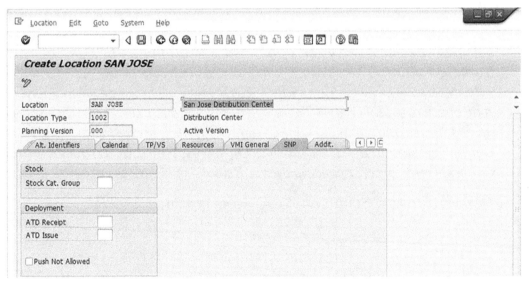

The stock category group and the available-to-deploy (ATD) receipt are shown on this tab. The ATD issue fields can be assigned at a location or at a product location. Often these fields are assigned at a location because they apply for all products at the location.

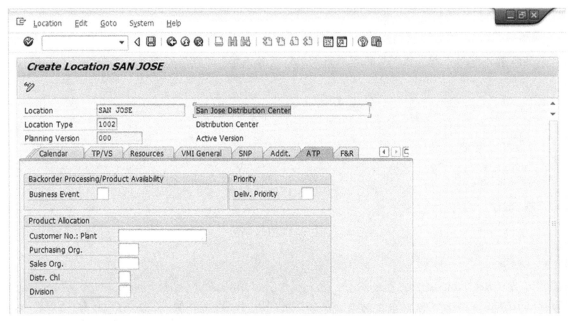

This tab is used for GATP and is where the following fields are entered. Essentially these fields assign the location to various things that are primarily on the ERP side. Therefore, a location in APO can be assigned to an ERP Sales Org, Distribution Channel—things that do not exist in APO:

- *Business Event: A selection of defined operations within an enterprise's working routine. The selected business event triggers the ATP check (i.e., sale, receipt of order, shipment). —SAP Help—This determines when the ATP check actually occurs. There are many options here. A few examples are: an SD (Sales and Distribution) Order, SD Order; make-to-stock, SD Order; vendor consignment, SD Delivery, On hand, Stock in Transfer, Planned Orders, Creation of a process order, Release of a process order.*

- *Delivery Priority: Simply another way to prioritize GATP.*

- *Customer No: Plant: Customer assigned to the plant for the purposes of the stock transport order. —SAP Help*

- *Sales Organization: Organizational unit responsible for the marketing and sale of certain products or services. The responsibility assumed by a sales organization may include legal responsibility for products and customers' rights of recourse.*

- *Distribution Channel: Channel through which goods or services reach the customer. Typical examples of distribution channels are the wholesale and retail trades and direct sales. —SAP Help*

- *Division: Grouping of materials, products, and services. By reference to the division, the system determines the sales and business areas to which a material, a product, or a service is assigned. A division can represent a certain product group, for example. Through the grouping of several products under a division, it is possible data is valid for the area of a division. You can restrict price agreements entered into with a customer to a certain division, for example. You can also create sales statistics at division level and carry out marketing activities (such as a direct mailing campaign). —SAP Help*

Location Types

When a location is created in APO, it must be created as a particular type of location. The location type not only identifies what the location is for users, but also determines what the location can do. The location types control how the location behaves and what the location is capable of doing. In the screen shot below, you can see the other location types available within APO:

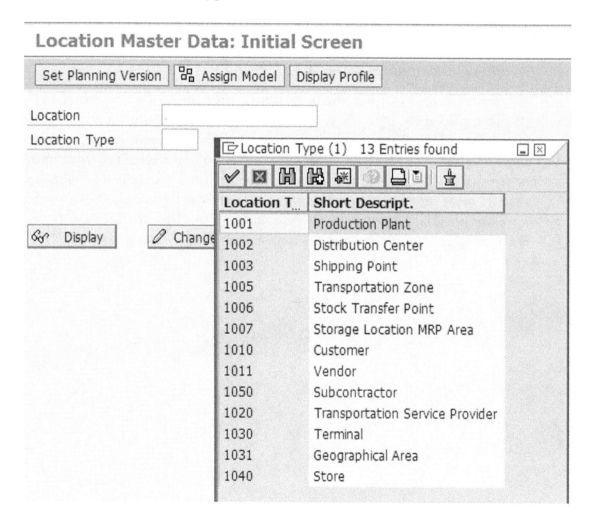

Location Master Data: Initial Screen

Set Planning Version | 🔲 Assign Model | Display Profile

Location

Location Type

Location Type (1)   13 Entries found

Location T...	Short Descript.
1001	Production Plant
1002	Distribution Center
1003	Shipping Point
1005	Transportation Zone
1006	Stock Transfer Point
1007	Storage Location MRP Area
1010	Customer
1011	Vendor
1050	Subcontractor
1020	Transportation Service Provider
1030	Terminal
1031	Geographical Area
1040	Store

Display | Change

The following types of locations can be set up and used in SAP APO:

1. 1001: Production Plant

2. 1002: Distribution Center

3. 1003: Shipping Point

4. 1005: Transportation Zone

5. 1006: Stock Transfer Point

6. 1007: Storage Location MRP Area

7. 1010: Customer

8. 1011: Vendor

9. 1050: Subcontractor

10. 1020: Transportation Service Providers

11. 1030: Terminal

12. 1031: Geographic Area

13. 1040: Store

More on location types can be found at the following links:

http://www.scmfocus.com/sapplanning/2009/04/10/scm-location-types/

http://www.scmfocus.com/sapplanning/2012/07/05/location-types-in-sap-apo/

Locations are normally brought over from SAP ERP, as is shown in the core interface screen shot below:

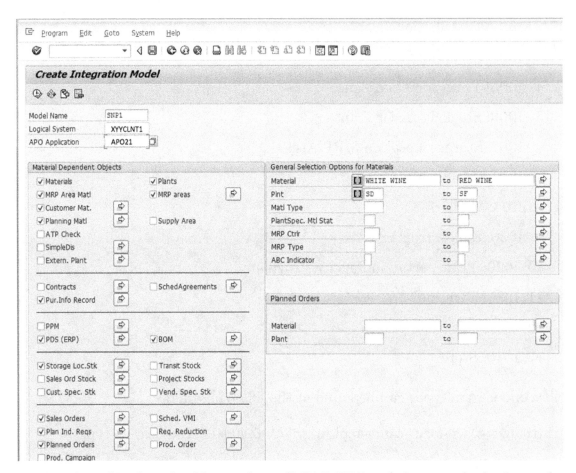

The core interface has checkboxes that tell SAP ERP to bring over both plants that become locations in APO, as well as other nonphysical locations in SAP ERP, such as MRP Areas. The logic for creating the locations in SAP ERP and then bringing them over to APO is that eventually all of the activity that takes place in each APO location is communicated to a location counterpart in SAP ERP.

While locations are generally (but not in all circumstances) brought over from SAP ERP, there are still fields that must be populated from APO.

Create Integration Model

Material Dependent Objects				General Selection Options for Materials			
☐ Materials		☐ Plants		Material		to	⇨
☐ MRP Area Matl		☐ MRP areas	⇨	Plnt		to	⇨
☐ AMPL				Matl Type		to	⇨
☐ Customer Mat.	⇨			PlantSpec. Mtl Stat		to	⇨
☐ Planning Matl	⇨	☐ Supply Area		MRP Ctrlr		to	⇨
☐ ATP Check				MRP Type		to	⇨
☐ SimpleDis	⇨			ABC Indicator		to	⇨
☐ Extern. Plant	⇨						

				Selection of Source of Supply			
☐ Contracts	⇨	☐ SchedAgreements	⇨	☐ Material-Dependent Source of Supply Selection			
☑ Pur.Info Record	⇨			☐ Include Dependent Vendors and Issuing Plants			
☐ PPM	?			Vendor		to	⇨
☐ PDS (ERP)	?	☐ BOM	⇨	Create Loc./BP			
				Material		to	⇨
☐ Storage Loc.Stk		☐ Transit Stock	⇨	Supplying Plant		to	⇨
☐ Sales Ord Stock		☐ Project Stocks	⇨	Selection of Purchasing Info Record			
☐ Cust. Spec. Stk		☐ Vend. Spec. Stk	⇨	Vendor		to	⇨
				Material		to	⇨
☐ Sales Orders	⇨	☐ Sched. VMI	⇨	Purch. Org		to	⇨
☐ Plan Ind. Reqs	⇨	☐ Req. Reduction		Plnt		to	⇨
☐ Planned Orders	⇨	☐ Prod. Order	⇨	Info Rec. No.		to	⇨
☐ Prod. Campaign				☐ Standard Info Record			
☐ POs and PReqs	⇨	☐ Manual Reserv.		☐ Subcontracting Info Record			
				☐ Consignment Info Record			
☐ Insp. Lots							

Choice of Type

Purchase Info Records are brought into APO and vendors automatically created locations.

Suppliers are created from Purchasing Info Records from SAP ERP. A supplier location can be brought in as a standard supplier, a subcontract location, or as a consignment location. Subcontract locations and consignment locations, which we will address in other chapters, add considerable complexity to the supply network because both of these locations are pseudo internal locations; that is, they are internal locations in some regards and external locations in others. APO, and in fact many other supply chain planning suites, do not work smoothly with pseudo internal locations. The supplier is then shown as a vendor type, which can be listed as location types above. If you go back up to the location type listing, they are the three location types with asterisks by them.

ERP Locations

Now that we have covered the location types in SAP APO, we can cover the location types in SAP ERP, which are as follows:

1. Plant

2. Customer Location

3. Supplier

4. DC

What should be immediately apparent is that there are far fewer location types in SAP ERP than in APO. But if locations begin their life in SAP ERP and are brought over to APO, how can so few locations in SAP ERP result in so many different locations in APO? Good question! One reason is that many geographic entities that are not locations in SAP ERP become locations once they are brought into APO. For instance, an MRP Area is a specific area within a location in SAP ERP. They can be used to represent storage locations, which of course is not a "location." However, within APO they become a location with the location type 1007. The same applies for this shipping point. Obviously a shipping point is an area within a location where loading onto transportation equipment occurs. But in APO, a shipping point is a location type 1003.

I can't say for sure why SAP followed this approach with regard to locations, which is a different approach to the one used with SAP ERP. I don't see any real advantage to setting up everything as a location in APO, and there are some disadvantages because now translation is necessary every time one speaks to an ERP resource; however, it is not of much consequence. Mainly it's important to understand that APO locations are simply managed differently than in SAP ERP.

It would be a very rare project that would use all of the location types available within APO. Setting up the location as a particular location type changes the behavior of the location; most importantly, the movement types are created. On some occasions it makes sense to use a different location type from the one that would be assumed by looking at the descriptions, because the requirements mean modeling the supply network in a nonstandard way. Therefore, the location types can be seen as a series of options with particular attributes available to the designer.

Distribution Center

Distribution centers (DCs) are stock holding locations in the supply network. Companies have different types of DCs. They often have larger regional distribution centers (RCDs), which are fed by manufacturing locations and which then feed what they call DCs—normally the layer prior to the customer. (This is of course a generalization. There are many different possible supply network designs. For instance, some companies only distribute and do manufacturing). However, APO does not differentiate between distribution center types. A DC and RDC would both be set up as the 1002: Distribution Center location type.

Production Plant

Production plants manufacture product and store stock. Planned (production) orders are created by APO in the factories that are eventually converted to production orders.

Customer

Customer locations are of course the final destination of all products. The fact that customers are set up as locations is a bit inconsistent. Normally vendors are not set up as locations, and neither customer locations nor suppliers are considered part of the internal supply network. Whenever a location that is not inside the supply network is modeled as a location, more work results in the form of increased master data setup and additional maintenance. But it also means more visibility into that location.

Vendor/Supplier Locations

Vendors can be modeled as locations, but this is not a requirement. However, APO will have little information about vendors that are not modeled,. Vendors can be set up as locations when the company wants to do the following:

1. View supplier capacities

2. Constrain the vendor production on the basis of constrained resources

3. Use the transportation load builder to build loads from the vendor to the company's own internal locations

When a vendor is modeled as a location the lead-time is determined from a transportation lane. When a vendor is not modeled as a location, the planning delivery time in days is taken from the Procurement Tab on the Product Location Master. This is relevant Procurement Types below with an asterisk:

1. *External Procurement (Brought in from a vendor)

2. In-house Production (Produced internally)

3. *External or In-house Production (The system has the option of either bringing in the material from a vendor or producing the item in-house.)

4. External Procurement Planning (It's hard to know how SAP could have made this option description more confusing, but the word "external" here does not refer to external to the supply network. Instead, external here means external to APO. So the product is planned in the ERP system.)

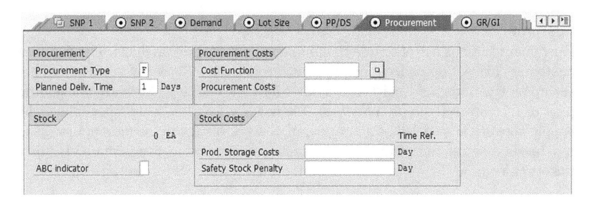

In most cases modeling a vendor as a location is done for just a portion of the vendor database, as it is more effort to set up and to manage. In addition, the desire to perform the above activities is limited to a certain set of vendors, such as those with the largest volumes or with the most critical products. Secondly, there are several ways to model vendors. The most important distinction is whether or not the vendor is capacity-constrained. In cases where the vendor is not capacity-constrained (which could be because of the supply planning method used, or because of an active choice to not capacity-constrain the vendors), then the vendor location is used more for capacity visibility.

The capacity constraining options for a vendor location are mostly the same as for an internal location, except that the options for the technical objects that can represent the capacity are fewer. I have also come across large companies with few vendors that modeled every single vendor as a location, something that is generally only feasible for those companies with few vendors.

http://www.scmfocus.com/sapplanning/2012/10/12/capacity-constraining-supplier-location-in-snp/

Shipping Point Location
Shipping Point Location is used with TP/VS, so I will not cover this location in this book.

Transportation Zone
The location can be used to group multiple customers into a transportation zone. The main purpose for creating a transportation zone is to decrease the number of transportation lanes that are created. Transportation lanes are actually complex master data objects that require quite a bit of maintenance. Transportation lanes are covered in Chapter 3: "Transportation Lanes." Transportation zones are also used for TP/VS.

Stock Transfer Point
This location type is not documented well and I have never seen it actually used on a project.

Storage Location MRP Area
MRP Areas provide significant flexibility within the physical location. This location type is covered in detail in Chapter 5: "Managing Storage Locations with MRP Areas for Allocation and Global Available to Promise (GATP)."

Subcontractor

This location type is used to support the subcontracting processing APO. Subcontractor locations are tricky because they are a pseudo internal location. The relationship between a subcontractor location and an internal location in APO involves both a purchase requisition (which is an external document) as well as a stock transport requisitions (which is an internal movement type).

Transportation Service Providers

This is a location for use by TP/VS so I will not cover it in this book.

Terminal and Geographic Area and Store

These are three location types that I have yet to see used or even discussed on a project.

Conclusion

How locations are set up in APO was a natural starting point for a book on setting up the APO supply network. Each location within APO is set up with a Location Master. The Location Master controls the behavior of the location and has a series of tabs for categories of control. These tabs are: General, Address, Calendar, VMI, SNP and ATP. When a location is created in APO, it must be set up as a specific location type. APO has quite a few location types, only half of which are generally used on projects. Usually locations are brought over from SAP ERP into APO from the CIF; however, master data setup must still take place once the locations have been brought into APO, as some of the data for the locations is referred to as APO-maintained data. As such, there are some fields that do not have any meaning in SAP ERP. Furthermore, while some locations are actual "locations" in ERP, a number of other entities that come across to APO through the CIF as locations are not actual locations in SAP ERP.

Locations can be assigned priorities so that some locations receive preferential stocking and service level attainment over other locations. In supply planning, location priorities only work with the CTM supply planning method. This is just one of the prioritization types available within SNP. This chapter covered the Location, Product, PPM/PDS, the Distribution, and the Procurement priorities.

CHAPTER 3

Transportation Lanes

Transportation lanes are the second major master data object after the location. It determines how material will flow through the supply network. Frequently, a transportation lane is described as a lane between two locations. That is its general definition outside of SAP, and works well enough most of the time when discussing SNP. However, there are actually several variations of a transportation lane, which are important to understand and which can be seen clearly in the transportation lane setup. Therefore, a transportation lane is all of the following:

1. A relationship between two locations

2. A relationship between two locations for a particular product

3. A relationship between two locations for a Means of Transport (MOT)

4. A relationship between two locations for a Transportation Service Provider

Transportation lanes connect locations, but transportation lanes do not connect all location types. For instance, shipping points and MRP areas are within locations that are already connected to other locations by transportation lanes. Conversely, some locations that are not real physical locations are connected to other locations with transportation lanes. This will be explained in Chapter 6: "Intercompany Transfer Locations." Transportation lanes are created automatically in APO through the CIF when Scheduling Agreements, Contracts or Purchasing Info Records (supplier records) exist in the SAP ERP system. This is shown in the screen shot below:

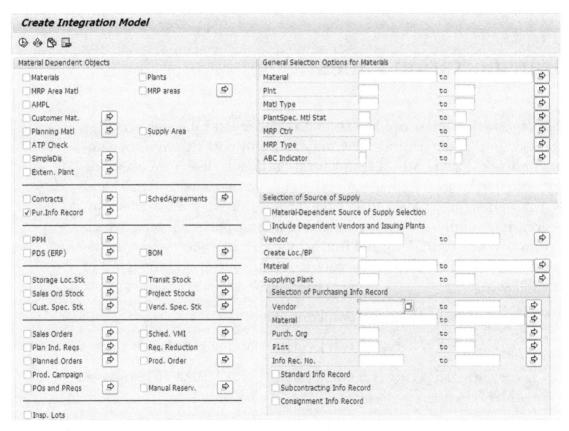

When one selects the Purchasing Info Record button, the options to the right appear and the transportation lanes are created only for the selections that are entered.

However, when internal locations are brought into APO through the CIF, transportation lanes are not created; they must be manually created instead.

Transportation lanes have a large number of fields, which are designed to meet a wide variety of functionality needs with only a subset of these related to supply network design. It is likely that an implementation will only activate a small number of these fields, but for our purposes you should understand all the fields or at least those related to supply planning. I have reviewed all of the fields in the transportation lanes and organized them into the following categories:

1. *Time Horizon, Calendar and Timing Related Fields:* Transportation lanes have quite a few timing fields. However, none of the timing fields are pertinent for supply planning design. Furthermore, I cover these fields extensively, as well as all other time horizon, calendar and timing fields across the four most commonly implemented APO modules—DP, SNP, GATP and PP/DS—in my book, *Planning Horizons, Calendars and Timings in SAP APO.*[5]

2. *TLB Related Fields:* Those related to controlling the behavior of the transportation load builder (TLB)—some of which are also timing related fields.

3. *Resource Related Fields:* While not often employed, transportation resources can be used and even constrained in SNP. However, it very rarely is. More on this topic is covered in this article:

   http://www.scmfocus.com/supplyplanning/2011/10/02/commonly-used-and-unused-constraints-for-supply-planning/

4. *Cost Related Fields:* For use by the SNP Optimizer.

5. *SPP Related Fields:* Some of the fields on the transportation lane are used by a parallel supply planning application to SNP called SPP (service parts planner). This application is unrelated to SNP and is customized for the service parts industry—combining both supply planning and demand planning for the unique planning needs of service parts. I will not cover SPP fields in this book, but you can learn more about SPP in the articles located at the following link:

   http://www.scmfocus.com/sapplanning/category/spp/

---

[5] One could say that the timing field, "Transport Duration of a Transportation Lane," could be included in the set up of the supply network, as the duration determines how far locations are from one another. However, I am not going to follow that approach as I categorize that as a timing field, and I will not cover timing fields in this book.

6. *Fields for Setting Up the Supply Network:* These fields are relevant to our purposes here, and are listed and described below. Three different types of transportation lanes that can be set up in APO:

   a. *Transportation Lane Header*: This is basic information to establish the connection between two locations.

   b. *Product Specific Transportation Lane:* A transportation lane can be valid for all products or valid for only some products. Products that are not valid for a transportation lane are excluded from the Product Specific Transportation Lane. On the other hand, different values (such as different transportation costs, lot size profiles, stacking factories, etc. can be applied to different products along the same transportation lane. The fields can have different values per product by creating different product-specific transportation lanes. When there is no desire to differentiate among products, and no need to exclude products per transportation lane, there is no need to create product-specific transportation lanes. Instead a company can set up either multiple—or even a single—means of transport and not create product-specific transportation lanes.

   c. *Means of Transport (MOT):* The mode of transportation (rail, truck, air, ship, etc.), as well as the equipment (twenty-foot container, forty-foot container, etc.) that is valid along the Product Specific Transportation Lane.

   d. *Product Specific Means of Transport:* These are the fields that are relevant for that means of transport for the specific product. This has the fewest fields of the three different transportation lane settings and in fact at many companies is not even used.

Judging by how many times the transportation lane setup has to be explained on projects, transportation lanes are one of the more challenging master data objects or set of master data objects (depending on how you look at it) in APO. The screen shots on the following page are designed to explain how transportation lanes are set up.

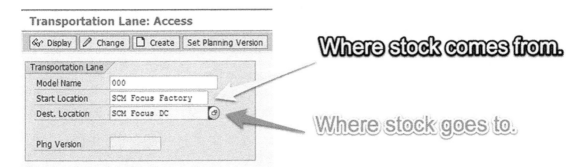

To begin, we will need to choose a model name, a start location and destination location.

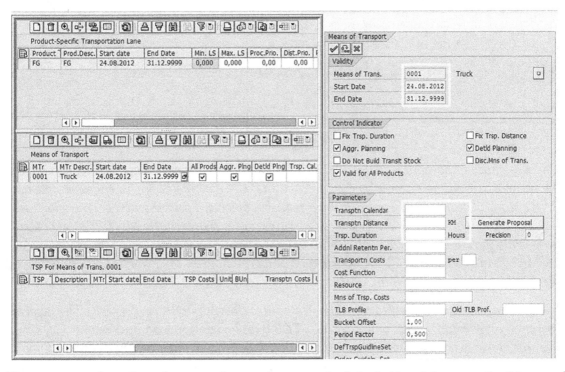

Here we are selected on the second pane down on the left. In the right pane the Means of Transport (MOT) view is shown. The MOT represents a specific piece of transportation equipment.

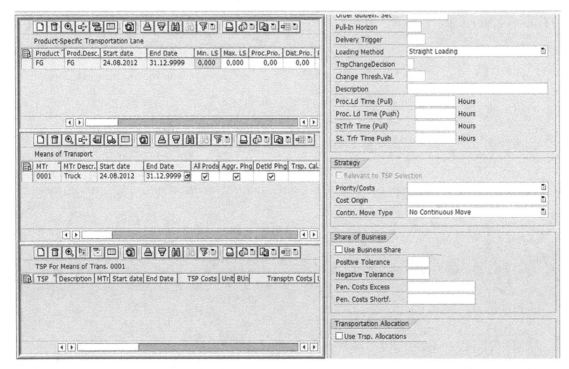

One misleading aspect of transportation lanes is that it seems as if the MOT is created in the transportation lane user interface. In fact it is only assigned here, in conformance with SAP's standard approach to assignment between objects. I find the MOT Transportation Lane to be a relatively misleading configuration area. Between the MOT Transportation Lane and the MOT (which I will show below), there are seventy-seven fields. However, only two fields on the MOT Transportation Lane are also on the externally-defined MOT: the Means of Transport Name and the MTr Description.

When an object is assigned to a profile, its values do not populate a screen. The object is assigned to a profile in the same way as a TLB (transportation load builder) profile, except that all of the MOT information shows in this screen. The various MOTs are defined in a different transaction (shown on the following page), and actually are assigned to the transportation lane header. A MOT can be valid for all products, or can be specific to one product.

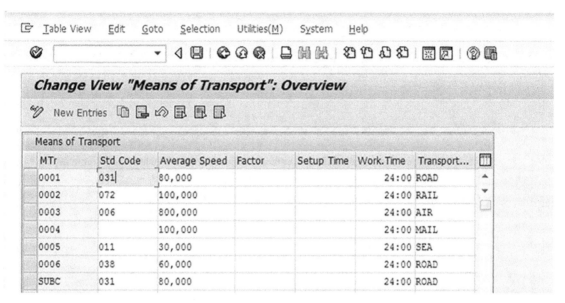

Here is where the MOTs are defined.

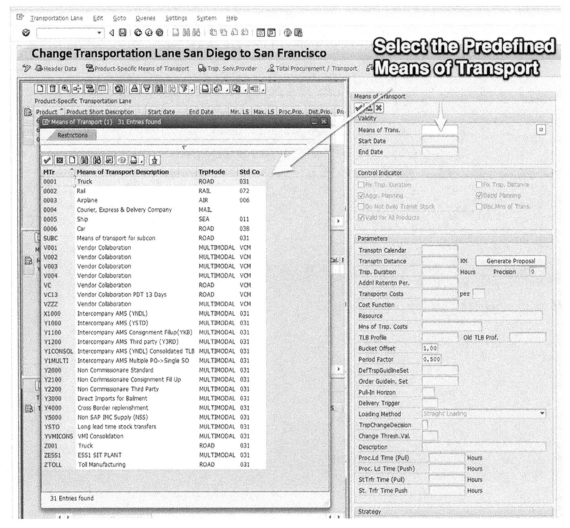

Once the MOT is defined, you can go into the transportation lane transaction and assign it to a transportation lane header.

The next step is to create the product-specific transportation lanes, which define the source of supply in the system—essentially a series of switches, which set up the valid location-to-location combinations in the network. Product-specific transportation lanes can be blocked or unblocked, allowing the sources of supply to be changed very quickly. Changing the blocking indicator is very easy to do, and some clients create a customized procedure that reaches out and changes the blocking indicator based upon a table that is maintained by a group responsible for sourcing decisions. This solution turns out to be a far better way of managing multi-sourcing than attempting to activate the multi-sourcing functionality in APO. This is covered in Chapter 4: "Sources of Supply and Multi-sourcing."

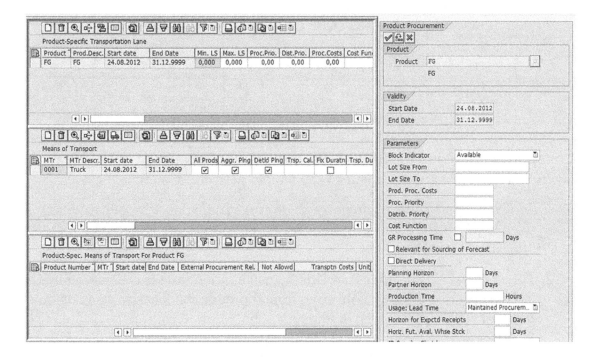

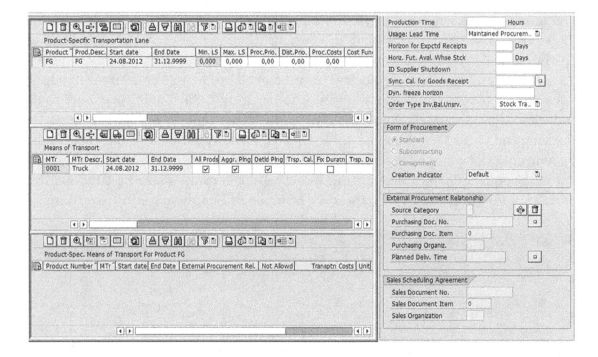

Transportation Fields for Setting Up the Supply Network
The following fields are pertinent to the supply network design:

1. *Indicator for Use in Aggregated Planning*: Indicates whether an entry is used in aggregated planning. Aggregated planning is covered in Chapter 2: "Locations in APO."

2. *Direct Delivery:* Specifies that this transportation lane is considered by the SNP heuristic for direct deliveries from a production location to a customer location. Thus, there is no detour via a distribution center (DC). This field is relevant to supply network design because it defines a different route that circumvents the DC.

3. *Source of Supply (i.e., Procurement Relationship Type):* Indicates the category of procurement relationship. The options are: contract, scheduling agreement or purchase info record. "Purchase info record" is the most common source of supply. The field is somewhat confusing because "source of supply"

typically means the location or locations from which the supply is being sourced (as in the "source of supply" described in Chapter 2: "Locations in APO"). Probably a better name for this field would be the "Procurement Relationship Type," because if you look at its definition that's exactly what it is.

4. *Distribution Priority (i.e., the Deployment Quantity):* The sequence determines where requirements in deployment are processed using the Fair Share Rule D. The distribution priority refers to the target location of the transportation lane. The highest priority is therefore priority "0." For instance, let's say that two target locations (A and B) each has a requirement of 100 pieces. In source location C, the available-to-deploy quantity (ATD quantity) is 150 pieces.[6] Location A has distribution priority 1 and location B has priority 2. In this case, location A would be assigned 100 pieces and location B the remaining fifty pieces.

5. *Procurement Priority:* Is used both by the initial supply plan and by the deployment plan. This field defines the priority of a source of supply in source determination. The highest priority is priority "0." In Production Planning and Detailed Scheduling, the system uses additional criteria for source determination, such as costs. If the procurement priority is the same, the system selects the source with the lower costs. For deployment, you use the procurement priority to determine the sequence of source locations from which *real time deployment* is started, if you are using this for a destination location. The SNP and deployment optimizers only take this

---

[6] For those unfamiliar with the term "available to deploy" (ATD), it is the planned stock-on-hand that is available to be sent from a location. It is similar in concept to the available-to-promise quantity (ATP), but instead of promising stock, it is the quantity to be sent. ATD is highly customizable and is assigned to the SNP 2 tab of the Location or the Product Location Master (that is, the ATD rule can be applied at both intersections). ATD is assigned to both the receipt field (what the product location can receive) and the issue field (what it can send). The ATD is used for both TLB and deployment. Of all the supply planning runs, the least emphasis tends to be placed on deployment and redeployment.

field into account if you use automatic cost generation,[7] and have set the indicator on the *Procurement Priority of PPMs/PDSs* or *Procurement Priority of Transportation Lanes* in the SNP or deployment optimization profile.

6. *Blocked Indicator for Source of Supply*: This blocks the use of the product-specific transportation lane (it is applied to the product-specific transportation lane). This field provides a great deal of flexibility to the configuration of the supply network. While we speak of "a supply network," in fact there are many supply networks. A product may be valid for every location, or may only be valid for a "subnetwork." When the Cost Optimizer is used, this is called "product decomposition," and is the main way the optimizer decomposes or divides the problem.[8] The blocked indicator can be adjusted in the transportation lane, or large numbers of product-specific transportation lanes can be updated using MASSD—the mass maintenance transaction in SAP APO. In this way the product-specific supply network—or the series of product-specific supply networks—can be very fluid and can change depending upon the time of year, special conditions, etc.

These six fields on the transportation lane(s) are the ones with which a supply network designer must be concerned, and are summarized in the following article:

http://www.scmfocus.com/sapplanning/2011/09/23/transportation-lane-settings/

---

[7] Automatic cost generation is important enough to have its own tab in the SNP Optimizer profile. In most cases, costs are entered into the optimizer explicitly. However, often this proves to be more complex than is thought and is something I have written about in the following article:

http://www.scmfocus.com/supplyplanning/2011/07/09/what-is-your-supply-planning-optimizer-optimizing/

Automatic cost generation ostensibly reduces this burden by allowing the company to instead set business goals by weighing them. You have the ability to weigh the priority of customer requirements, the priority of the corrected demand forecast, the priority of the demand forecast, the safety stock priority, as well as the priority of categories of products (A, B, C) all from a scale of 1 to 4. I cannot speak to the effectiveness of the automatic cost generation functionality within the SNP Optimizer as I have never seen it used, and have never been asked to investigate it by a client.

[8] Some people are surprised when I tell them that the SNP Cost Optimizer never provides an optimal solution for the supply network. Instead it provides a series of optimal solutions (or close to optimal depending upon the problem complexity, the hardware, and the amount of time given to the optimizer to run) for a series of subnetworks, as described in full detail in *Supply Planning with MRP, DRP and APS Software*.

Different Location Modeling within APO versus ERP

In order to meet requirement, some companies model differently in APO than SAP ERP. This lends significant complexity to the implementation which I cover in this section.

Background on Planning versus Execution in Location-to-Location Movements

On the surface, how transportation lanes are created in APO can seem straightforward. The basic concept is that any valid location-to-location combination is set up as a transportation lane. Source of supply can be controlled with either quota arrangements or priorities. Quota arrangements and priorities can also be used for PPMs and PDSs and these methods of controlling source of supply are referred to throughout the book so here is a good point to define them.

1. Quota Arrangement: This is a way of allocating a certain percentage of demand to different sources. For instance, 75 percent of demand over a particular time interval sourced from location A, 25 percent sourced from location B.

2. Priorities: Here a source of supply is used by the system before other sources of supply. For instance, location A as a primary source of supply, and location B as a secondary source of supply. The secondary source of supply would only be selected when the primary source of supply cannot meet the demand.

I will not get into multi-sourcing with the SNP Optimizer in this book because it's a distraction, but I do cover the topic in the following article:

http://www.scmfocus.com/supplyplanning/2011/07/14/the-false-assumption-of-multi-sourcing-in-cost-optimization/

The Importance of Incorporating Reality into a Design

The previous paragraph on multi sourcing makes an important assumption and omits significant information. Omissions of this nature are almost universal in all published information on APO (except for on SAP message boards such as SNC.SAP.COM, where people facing problems in the field tell the real story). The omission to which I am referring is that the functionality described above is available to companies if (and it is a big if) they are willing to put in the considerable effort required to maintain all of the master data that enables the functionality. It certainly sounds logical that a company would be willing to expend this effort because the company wants the desired functionality—right? Unfortunately, it's not that simple.

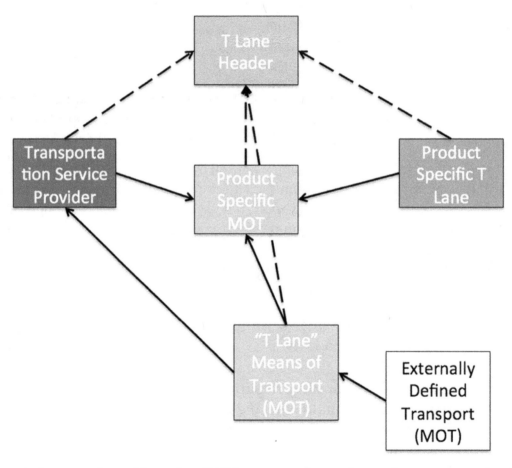

Transportation Lane Master Data Categories and Relationships

The set of master data objects that SAP has created to make up the transportation lane are complex and require a high level of maintenance. A transportation lane is made up of a variety of master data categories.

In just one of the transportation lane master data categories (the Means of Transport Transportation Lane)—combined with an externally determined master data object—and as I have already pointed out, there are seventy-seven fields in these transportation lanes. Transportation lanes in APO were not designed to be efficiently implemented or easily understood; they were designed to offer the maximum functionality and to allow SAP to say "yes we can do that" to more requirements during the sales process.

The complexity of transportation lanes prompts many companies to try to minimize the number of transportation lanes that they must maintain. For instance, many companies want to plan from one set of locations, but then in execution change the locations that are the source of supply. That is, they want to create confirmed stock transport requisitions (from deployment) from location A to destination B in APO, but eventually create a stock transport order from location B to destination C.

Stock Movement: Planning Versus Execution

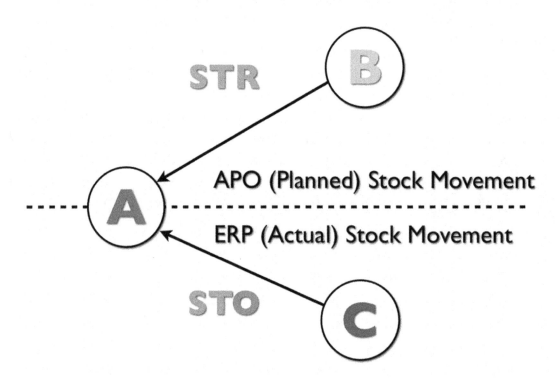

This is not the only example of a discrepancy of locations. Even within APO there can be differences between locations. For instance, some companies place forecasts onto locations within DP in a way that is different from how the supply will eventually be sourced. The demand planning department does not "care" where the product is sourced (location A or C), only that it is fulfilled from a location. The location B in this case may not even be a "real" location.

DP Versus SNP Forecast Assignment

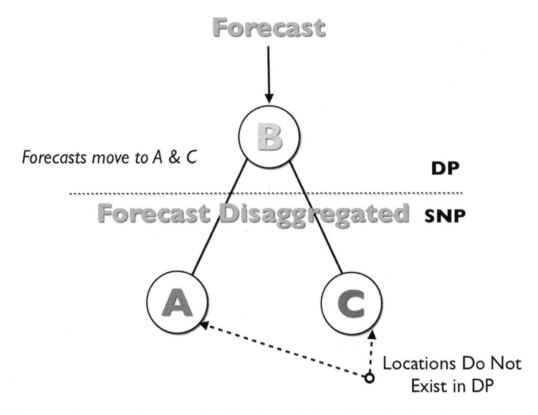

There can be several reasons for the above design. Not only do transportation lanes require significant maintenance, but more locations for DP means more characteristic value combinations (CVCs), which means more hardware space and more processing. Companies can reduce the number of CVCs by not forecasting the nonessential locations. In general, the maintenance effort required to fully represent reality is simply too overwhelming, and this is a shortcoming with APO. As a result, a variety of short cuts are often taken to reduce this overhead.

The Problem with the Design

While the design seems reasonable at first blush, APO is not designed to work with aggregated locations. APO is designed to have an STR created along a transportation lane and then to either create a matching STO along the transportation lane or receive an STO from SAP ERP along the same transportation lane. Errors will result if the STO and STR do not match across the transportation lane.

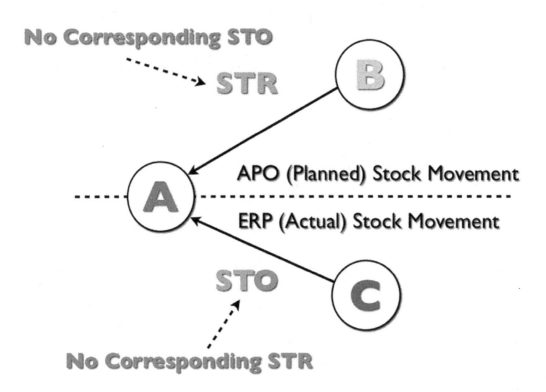

Stock Movement: Planning Versus Execution

How This Topic Dovetails with Redeployment

Interestingly, I ran into a similar issue related to mismatched STRs and STOs and discussed the topic in detail with another APO resource. The issue is essentially a subcategory of the topic of creating STOs in SAP ERP along transportation lanes, which do not match STRs that were created in APO, and the problem with reconciliation. Redeployment is a planning thread that does not exist in SNP (although it does exist in SPP), and most companies that implement SNP have some redeployment needs. Redeployment is explained in the following article:

http://www.scmfocus.com/inventoryoptimizationmultiechelon/2011/10/redeployment/

Redeployment is actually part of a larger topic, which I cover in *Multi Method Supply Planning in SAP APO*, and I am including only a small snippet of the overall topic here in order to show how the issue of unmatched STOs and STRs reoccurs in a variety of areas. Below is a quotation by the other APO resource from our discussion:

> *In order to reflect an externally-determined or manually-created redeployment, redeployment stock transport orders are necessary between DCs. This means transportation lanes must be set up in SNP in order for stock transport orders to come over from SAP ERP to SAP APO/SCM. This is true if STOs are created in SAP ERP. In fact, the CIF—which moves STOs from SAP ERP to SAP APO/SCM—will not be able to bring STOs over to SAP APO/SCM that are created in SAP ERP.*

http://www.scmfocus.com/sapplanning/2012/12/14/representing-a-partial-supply-network-in-apo-versus-sap-erp-and-stos/

Transportation Lead Times
Lead times are the time between locations to, within, or from, a supply network. Lead times are referred to as the "Transportation Duration" field, which was shown previously on the Means of Transport Transportation Lane.

Important Distinctions Between Supply Planning Systems
The assumptions of MRP, DRP, and all APS supply planning methods are based upon static lead times, that is, the lead-time stays the same regardless of the circumstance. (Unless updated.) However, with inventory optimization and multi-echelon planning software (MEIO), while the internal supply network lead times

are entered as static master data, MEIO can calculate adjustable effective lead times, which the system then uses to make more advanced decisions than are available to any other supply planning method. This is discussed in my book, *Inventory Optimization and Multi-Echelon Planning.*

Realistic Lead Times and the Need for Flexible Planning System Configuration

In addition to a definition of lead times, I think it's important to include a few features of how lead times are used in supply planning systems in practice. One of the major issues related to lot size determination is data quality and lead-time accuracy. For a supply planning system to calculate accurate dates, it must have lead times that reflect the reality of operations. The problem is that often the systems do not. Interestingly this issue is not discussed within companies, but it should be; it is a much wider problem than generally understood, and while there is a universal interest in forecast accuracy, lead-time accuracy is often overlooked.

Reasons Why Lead Times Can Be Inaccurate

1. Accurate measurements were never taken.

2. Lead times have changed from when the initial values were entered.

3. Active decision-making on the part of the company. Selecting a low production turnaround time, or a low supplier delivery lead time can feel good to executives or to departments trying to look good to higher-ups. However, if these values do not reflect reality, the plan will be in error. Planning works best when the model reflects the reality of the enterprise. Planning systems can handle anything, but they must be told the truth.

Lead Time Sampling Bias

It is important to control for sample bias in selecting lead times (selecting from an unrepresentative time of year, taking averages from small samples or batches with data integrity issues). It is important to recognize that industry delivery times can change. For example, several years ago, lead times for rare components such as titanium greatly increased due to a cyclical increase in the aerospace industry. At a client I worked with, the lead times in the system had not been modified to reflect these increased lead times. Updating the supply chain model is critical not only in lot sizes and lead times, but for resources as well as a number of planning parameters. Far too often, planning systems are implemented for the present circumstances, without the necessary configuration (which is more work of course) for the planning system to flex as the business environment changes.

Conclusion

Transportation lanes connect the various location types that are true physical locations in APO (rather than locations such as MRP Areas). On projects, transportation lanes end up consuming quite a bit of effort because they have so many fields, and because of the relatively confusing nature of how transportation lanes are set up. To help manage the complexity of transportation lanes, the transportation lane fields were organized in this chapter into the following categories: *Time Horizon, Calendar and Timing Related Fields, TLB Related Fields, Resource-related Fields, Cost-related Fields, SPP-related Fields, Fields for Setting Up the Supply Network, Means of Transport Fields, Product-specific Means of Transport Fields.*

Outside of SAP, a transportation lane is described frequently as a lane between two locations. Most of the time this definition works well enough when discussing SNP. However, there are actually several variations of a transportation lane that were defined in this chapter and are important to understand. The concept of different derivations of transportation lanes is already confusing, and the user interface for transportation lanes does nothing to alleviate the confusion. This chapter includes one of the more detailed explanations of transportation lanes available. I actually wrote part of it in order to explain transportation lanes to my own clients before using it in this book.

Transportation lanes control the flow of material through the supply network, and they have settings that can adjust the normal flow of material in order to bring about desired outcomes. Three ways of doing this are: assigning costs to transportation lanes (when the optimizer is used), using prioritization, and using quota arrangements.

In all the literature I have ever read about transportation lanes, the omission of how high in maintenance they are is glaring. All projects that I have worked on eventually attempt to limit the number of transportation lanes that are created for this very reason.

Issues with maintaining transportation lanes and other categories of master data prompt companies to take short cuts and to leave out things such as locations and transportation lanes from their APO models. These companies would prefer to create this master data if they had the wherewithal. When this happens there is a discrepancy between the master data of the supply network between APO and SAP ERP, and also a discrepancy in transactional data—as an example, STRs that are created in APO result in STOs that are created in ECC on different transportation lanes. This discrepancy creates a reconciliation problem because APO is designed to have matching STRs and STOs on transportation lanes. This problem of mismatched supply networks and mismatched STRs and STOs relates to many processes in APO. Increasingly I am finding that mismatched supply networks are quite common on APO projects, resulting in many challenges.

SNP is a system that uses static lead times. Supply planning systems, aside from multi-echelon applications, work in this manner. MEIO can calculate adjustable effective lead times, which the system then uses to make more advanced decisions than are available to any other supply planning method. Lead times are one of the most important assumptions of a supply planning system; however, given their importance, it can be surprising that the lead times—which are represented by the Transportation Duration field on the Means of Transport Transportation Lane—are not more accurate. Companies tend to spend minimal amounts of money or to invest little time on determining and keeping lead times accurate. For whatever reason, the accuracy of things such as forecasts is of great interest, while the accuracy of lead times, which are just as important in determining the accuracy of the plan, is not as interesting.

CHAPTER 4

Sources of Supply and Multi-Sourcing

The standard sources of supply in APO are:

1. Production from an internal location (production sources of supply are PPMs or PDSs)

2. Stock transfer from an internal location

3. Purchasing which is external to the supply network

All of the master data objects that control the source of supply determination have validity periods that allow the master data objects to be brought into and out of service based upon dates. This provides flexibility to sourcing of supply decisions along the planning horizon, but as with anything of this nature, it requires a high level of maintenance.

Inside a location there can be multiple PPMs/PDSs, which can serve as alternatives for the same product. Alternate PPMs/PDS can have different priorities so that some PPMs/PDSs are used before others, and some PPMs/PDSs are used only when other alternate PPMs/PDSs are not possible to be used.[9] PPMs/PDSs can also have quota arrangements set for them, so that a certain percentage of the demand to a location is allocated to different PPMs/PDSs.[10] [11]Source of supply for production is determined during the MPS planning run, and can be re-determined either with manual capacity leveling, or by using the SNP Capacity Leveling Heuristic. The following screen shot shows the Capacity Leveling Profile used in SNP.

---

[9] Either costs or actual priorities can be used depending upon the supply planning method, but in either case the effect is to prioritize some PPMs/PDSs over others. The SNP Heuristic and CTM can work off of priorities for either transportation lanes or PPMs/PDSs. The Optimizer works off of costs for both master data objects.

[10] Although not used very frequently, a quota arrangement on a PPM/PDS is interesting. Quota arrangements are typically used to control procurement in a way that is consistent with arrangements that a company has made with suppliers. However, SAP adopted the concept to PPMs/PDSs and stock transfers as simply another way to control source of supply, even though the quota arrangement is not based upon any arrangement made with suppliers.

[11] Quota arrangements allow a company to set the percentage of supply that will be shipped from a specific location. Therefore, if location A is supplied by location B and C, B can be set to supply 50 percent of the quantity of product ABC, and C can be set up in the quota to supply the other 50 percent. That is in the documentation. However, the quota arrangement functionality seems larger in print than what is actually in the quota arrangement configuration screen.

Supply Network Planning: Capacity Leveling

⊕ Display Logs

	From Date		To Date	
Planning Buckets Profile				

Object Selection

○ Selection Profile

    Selection Profile [   ] ⚒

◉ Manual Selection

Planning Version			
Product Number		to	⇨
Resource		to	⇨

Selection of Alternative Resources

☐ Alternative Resources

Parameter Selection

○ Parameter Profile

◉ Manual Parameter Selection

Method Parameter

Capacity Leveling Method	Heuristic Method ▾
Scheduling Direction	Forward Scheduling ▾
☐ Level Fixed Orders	
☐ Set Order Fixing	
☐ Raise Orders to Header Level	
Maximum Utilization	100,000
Order Prioritization	Without Priority ▾
Sort Sequence	Ascending ▾
Maximum Runtime (in Minutes)	

Production source determination can be performed in a single planning run, such as when the CTM or the SNP Network Optimizer is used, or in two passes, when capacity leveling is used to smooth out the peaks in planned production that is higher than capacity. When this occurs, demand is moved both to new PPMs/PDSs in the same period/ planning bucket or in different planning buckets.

In most cases the SNP Capacity Leveling Heuristic is used for capacity leveling. However, SNP also has an optimizer, which can be used by simply changing the capacity-leveling method selection in the profile, which is shown above. SNP provides quite a few options that control how the capacity leveling is performed.

This chapter will spend a good deal of time on alternate sources of supply during stock transfer and procurement. However, the alternative source of supply that is easiest to understand is alternate production sources of supply. Whether a product's source of supply is production or procurement can be conditional on internal capacity. This is the purpose of the External or In-House Production option on the Procurement Type field. Also, the approach used to select a source of supply very much depends upon the method that is used. Throughout this chapter I will explain different alternative approaches to determining source of supply depending upon whether the SNP Heuristic, CTM or the SNP Cost Optimizer is used. I will not get into detail about any of these methods beyond what is necessary to explain source of supply determination. For those interested in more detail on these methods, please see my book, *Supply Planning in MRP, DRP and APS Software.*

Purchasing and stock transfer sources of supply are controlled in the transportation lane. As discussed in Chapter 3, a transportation lane has both a Product Specific master data entry screen as well as a Product Specific Means of Transport master data entry screen. With this set up for every valid product-location combination, APO knows **which locations are the sources of supply that can be called upon to satisfy demand.** A product-location combination can have one or multiple sources. When dealing with multiple sources, there are two ways of determining the source:

1. The source can be determined manually. When a manual entry is made in a planning book with a multi-source product location, a pop-up window will appear and the planner can make the multi-source decision on the fly.

2. Automatically by the APO.

In order to create a stock transport requisition, a source of supply must be set up in the system. The first level of "source of supply" is determined by the procurement type which was covered in Chapter 2: "Locations in APO." The source of supply determination can be seen as a hierarchy. At the top of the hierarchy are the quota arrangements. After the quota arrangements, the following mechanisms are used to perform the selection:

1. *Procurement Priority*: Sources of supply can be coded with priorities which take over if no quota is set. This transportation lane field was discussed in detail in Chapter 3: "Transportation Lanes."

2. *Costs*: When priorities are identical, the low cost source will be selected over the higher cost source.

3. *Procurement Type*: Here, in-house production is given precedence over procurement, if the same item can be either bought or made.

For background on how SNP Optimizer works with the source of supply, see the following article:

http://www.scmfocus.com/sapplanning/2009/05/05/source-of-supply-in-scm/

How Sources of Supply are Controlled in APO
Source of supply applies to the following modules in SAP APO:

1. SNP

2. CTM

3. PPDS

APO defines different sources of supply that can be selected automatically or in interactive planning. Inherent to this process is a method of prioritizing the different sources.

I will discuss two planning threads: the network planning thread (also known as the MPS or initial supply plan) and the deployment thread. Each is defined below, along with other planning threads:

1. S&OP and Rough Cut Capacity Plan: These are long-range planning threads and generally are not part of the live environment. They are used for analytical purposes rather than to drive recommendations to the ERP system.

2. *The Initial Supply Plan (performed by MRP in ERP systems): Produces the initial production and procurement plan. Is focused on bringing stock into the supply network, and in creating stock with planned production orders. Can also be called the master production schedule (MPS), if the initial supply plan is run under certain criteria. See the following article:

http://www.scmfocus.com/supplyplanning/2011/10/02/
the-four-factors-that-make-up-the-master-production-schedule/

3. *The Deployment Plan (performed by DRP in ERP systems): Focused on pushing stock from locations at the beginning of the supply network to the end of the supply network.

4. The Redeployment Plan (performed by specialized applications with redeployment functionality or with a custom report): Focused on repositioning stock, which is already in the supply network, to locations where it has a higher probability of consumption. See the following article:

http://www.scmfocus.com/inventoryoptimizationmultiechelon/2011/10/
redeployment/

In this book I will cover only the threads above that are preceded by an asterisk. I don't cover the S&OP or Rough Cut Capacity Planning threads because they use simply aggregated versions of the supply network planning thread. I do not cover the redeployment thread because redeployment functionality does not exist in SNP. The specific method available in SNP differs depending upon the thread. We will begin with the network planning thread.

The Supply Network Planning Thread

The supply network planning thread primarily creates planned production orders and purchase requisitions. It also creates unconfirmed stock transport requisitions, which are primarily designed to tie together the demand. The demand is distributed through the supply network based upon the cascading demand through each location.

The Hierarchy/Sequence of Source of Supply Determination for the SNP Heuristic and CTM

Implementing quotas in SCM are a way of ensuring that planning is in concert with the business arrangements that the company has made with its suppliers. The source of supply determination can be seen as a hierarchy.

1. *Quota Arrangements*: At the top of the hierarchy are the quota arrangements.

2. *Procurement Priority*: Procurement priority of the PPM/PDS or of the transportation lane (sources of supply can be coded with priorities which take over if no quota is set).

3. *Costs*: When priorities either do not exist or are identical, the low-cost source will be selected over the higher-cost source.

4. *Procurement Type*: Here, in-house production is given precedence over procurement, if the same item can be either bought or made.

The Hierarchy/Sequence of Source of Supply Determination for CTM

1. *Search Strategy*: Search strategy is assigned to the CTM Profile. A Search Strategy may be Stock, Manufacturing, and then Purchase. Therefore, the system first attempts to meet demand with planned stock, then from production, and finally it begins to plan procurement. All of this is used by CTM with the consideration, of course, to first meet all demand on time. CTM has a wide variety of tools for creating priorities.

2. *Quota Arrangements*: Next CTM looks to the quota arrangements.

3. *Procurement Priority*: Procurement priority of the PPM/PDS or of the transportation lane (sources of supply can be coded with priorities, they take over if no quota is set).

4. *Costs*: When priorities either do not exist or are identical, the low-cost source will be selected over the higher-cost source.

5. *Procurement Type*: Here, in-house production is given precedence over procurement, if the same item can be either bought or made.

The Hierarchy/Sequence of Source of Supply Determination: The SNP Network Optimizer and Sources of Supply

In previous versions, the SNP Optimizer did not respect these quotas and external procurement relationships. Supposedly in later releases it can, at least according to the release notes. However, I would be remiss if I did not mention that I have run into problems getting the optimizer to respect values other than costs.

http://www.scmfocus.com/supplyplanning/2012/01/03/the-problem-with-cost-optimization/

http://www.scmfocus.com/sapplanning/2011/07/14/attempting-fair-share-distribution-with-the-cost-optimizer/

And this is a major problem in APO: The releases notes state that functionality works a certain way that in reality does not work. Functionality will stay broken for years and SAP will do nothing to fix it, as this article describes:

http://www.scmfocus.com/sapplanning/2013/02/01/parallel-processing-for-the-snp-cost-optimizer/

Therefore, I can say that contrary to the literature provided by SAP, the more the company wants to apply non cost-oriented criteria for controlling source of supply, the less it should consider using the optimizer. Therefore, the more pre-existing quota arrangements and other agreements must be used, the less sense it makes to use the optimizer. Quota arrangements and external procurement relationships are the required procurement constraints in some industries. The logic is that better prices and quality can be obtained by signing these long-term agreements. This is true for a number of industries. The SNP Optimizer enables an approach that considers the marketplace, and makes decisions based upon costs (although it can also now respect quota arrangements); however, a cost-based approach works better for procurement situations that are not subject to significant scale economies, where the quality is relatively standardized, and where the items are more like commodities. This would include such industries as petro-chemical and agricultural post-processing.

The Deployment Planning Thread
Deployment follows the MPS or initial supply plan and creates the confirmed stock transport orders between the internal locations of the supply network.

The Hierarchy/Sequence of Source of Supply Determination for the SNP Heuristic

The SNP Deployment Heuristic uses quota arrangements and priorities on the transportation lanes in conjunction with fair share rules. The fields that control deployment for the Deployment Heuristic are spread out in numerous places in the SNP 2 tab of the Product Location Master. Why they are not all part of the SNP Deployment Profile has never made any sense to me. The fields are shown in the following screen shot:

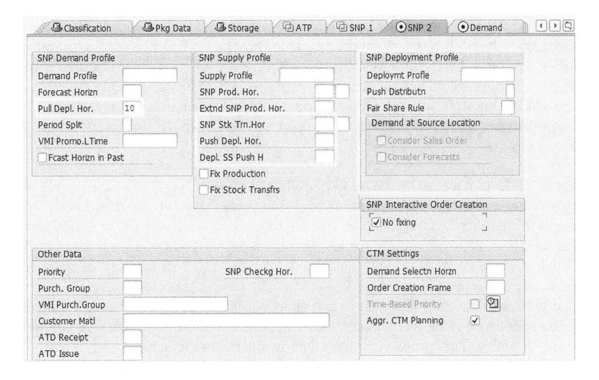

I have found that the SNP Deployment Heuristic works quite dependably. However, it only meets relatively basic customer requirements, which is why I have been on several projects that required custom deployment solutions.

The Hierarchy/Sequence of Source of Supply Determination for CTM
This is actually more of a placeholder because CTM is not used for deployment. Deployment can be performed with either the cost optimizer or with the deployment heuristic, although I have never seen the CTM network supply run deployed with anything but the deployment heuristic or with a custom solution.

The Hierarchy/Sequence of Source of Supply Determination for the SNP Optimizer and Sources of Supply
Many clients use the SNP Deployment Optimizer. In fact, the companies that I know use the SNP Network Optimizer also use the SNP Deployment Optimizer along with the SNP Network Optimizer. One way the SNP Deployment Optimizer differs from the SNP Network Optimizer is that it does not adjust planned (production) orders. So it simply accepts the planned (production) orders that were created by the SNP Network Optimizer as stable. However, the SNP Deployment Optimizer has extra parameters for deployment that the SNP Network Optimizer does not have.

The SNP Deployment Optimizer deploys based upon costs. It uses costs such as those assigned to the transportation lane, and trades them off against other costs (e.g., storage costs). Costs, such as storage costs between the sending and receiving locations, determine if the deployment tendency will be to either push or pull. (Push deployment moves stock out of a sending location in advance of planned demand, while pull deployment keeps stock at the sending location until there is a planned demand.) However, when there are competing needs the optimizer tends to send all of the stock to one location, which is not the way most companies want to deploy. This problem is described in the following article:

http://www.scmfocus.com/supplyplanning/2012/01/03/the-problem-with-cost-optimization/

Instead, most companies want to fair share their deployment so that multiple locations receive a portion of their demand under conditions of shortage. This is why SAP added fair share functionality to the SNP Deployment Optimizer, as shown in the following screen shot:

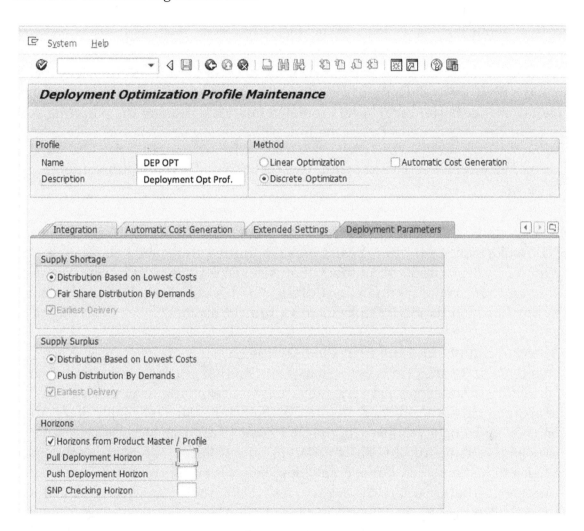

So the SNP Deployment Optimizer can work on costs. In theory, it can also work on fair share rules. However, in testing I was never able to get the fair share rules to work, as explained, in the following article:

http://www.scmfocus.com/sapplanning/2008/10/11/snp-deployment-and-fair-share/

SAP sells a fair share patch that I have tested. Its output made no sense to me because it simply gets the optimizer to disregard rounding values. I suggest that companies review the output of the SNP Deployment Optimizer very closely and perform extensive testing before they decide to use it.

The SNP Deployment Optimizer Profile uses different discrete horizon constraints than the SNP Network Optimizer Profile. The discrete horizon constraints control how far out the optimizer respects rounded quantities during the planning run. Discrete horizons are covered in the link below:

http://www.scmfocus.com/sapplanning/2013/02/19/discrete-optimization-horizon/

So, while the SAP documentation makes many definitive statements about the SNP Deployment Optimizer, I can't make definitive statements about using the optimizer for deployment except to say that it can deploy based upon costs. However, I suggest that companies analyze carefully whether they actually want to deploy the way in which the SNP Deployment Optimizer deploys.

Source of Supply and the SNP Cost Optimizer

Often the SNP Cost Optimizer is sold as a system that provides a very high degree of flexibility to the supply network, adjusting to meet changing circumstances. In the abstract this is a nice idea; in practice, however, source of supply determination ends up being a weakness of the SNP Cost Optimizer because it frequently provides confusing and radically different output based upon extremely small changes to just one cost. For example, just before writing this book I was asked to review a situation where the location for which production was scheduled had changed. The change was due to a revised storage cost at a location that was connected to one of the production locations. The storage cost had been altered to test a separate issue; however, it ended up causing a problem in a different area, which required an analysis. I recommended that the transportation time on a transportation lane be adjusted (the optimizer adjusted the production location because of the interaction between the new storage cost and the transportation time, which was a strange result in my view). My suggestion rectified the issue, more or less. I should also point out that in this situation there was also a major weakness in the optimizer cost setup: there were no transportation costs in the transportation lane (the optimizer cost settings were ported from a region with a very simple supply network to a region with a more complex supply network without any review of the costs),[12] which caused the source of supply to switch erratically and even caused stock to be moved back and forth within the supply network.

A number of issues are intertwined here. One issue is that optimizer implementations are complex and very few people know how to implement them correctly. I cover this in the following article:

http://www.scmfocus.com/inventoryoptimizationmultiechelon/2011/05/how-costs-are-really-set-in-cost-optimization-implementations/

But SNP's optimizer makes it more difficult to implement than it really should be. Hopefully the previous example adequately highlighted the time-consuming troubleshooting that is required on optimization projects. Companies that want to run the SNP Optimizer in a way that adds value to the business (and is not just a trophy project) must willingly fund the many cycles of learning to tune the optimizer properly. A commitment to running the optimizer correctly means years of funding, in some cases pushing off successive go-lives in order to get the optimizer right. As for the optimizer being a flexible and advanced source of supply functionality (as is often promised during the sales phase of projects), I can say that while hypothetically possible, I have seen most companies struggle just to meet the basic source of supply requirements that they have. This leads into the next topic, which is multi-sourcing.

---

[12] The assumption on this project was that costs that had been used from one region could simply be ported to a new region, and that they would work fine to control the flow of material properly in that region. Secondly, the company had been live for years in the first region, and they had also invested significantly in tuning the optimizer for that region. Unfortunately once the new region was brought up on the optimizer, the costs should have been viewed as if it were a completely new implementation. However, because this issue was not recognized, no time was allotted to do this. I was actually told not to worry about costs in the new region because that issue had been worked out, and the first implementation had been designed to take into account the need of all the subsequent regions. It had not.

The Allure of Multi-sourcing

An interesting aspect of software selection is why companies select one method of supply planning over another. One major reason companies select cost optimization is to perform constraint-based planning. Another powerful motivation is to perform multi-sourcing. Constraint-based planning is the ability to restrict capacity, primarily in the production resources, although hypothetically companies either project or are told that they will constrain on the basis of other supply chain constraints such as transportation and warehousing.

Understanding Multi-sourcing

When there is more than one source and the sourcing is determined by the APO, the functionality is referred to as multi-sourcing. Multi-sourcing is the ability for a supply planning system to choose intelligently between alternate sources of supply. One common reason for multi-sourcing is to move to a second or even third location in order to satisfy the demand when the primary location cannot handle the capacity of the order. Another reason can be to spread, by rough percentages, the total demand among various supply sources. Although we have already reviewed different areas where multiple sources of supply can be selected by SNP, for whatever reason the term multi-sourcing refers to choosing from among multiple sources of supply for either a stock transfer or a procurement movement.

In theory, there are two methods for performing multi-sourcing in SNP. One is CTM and the other is the SNP Optimizer. How each method works with multi-sourcing is described below:

- Multi-sourcing with CTM: In addition to being able to pick from different sources, CTM can choose from among different alternative resources, both within a location and transportation PPMs/PDSs. Therefore, CTM is allowed to switch to a secondary resource/PPM/PDS if the first one is consumed. *However, that is a selection between resources within one location.* If there are two production lines that make the same product in two different factories, CTM cannot switch to a different factory, and cannot change the source of supply based upon a resource becoming consumed in the factory with the resource set to the top priority.

- Multi-sourcing with the SNP Optimizer: The SNP Optimizer does not perform multi-sourcing based upon the priority setting in the location master. Instead it bases multi-sourcing upon the relative costs. At least it works that way in theory. I have never seen a company that turned on the multi-sourcing functionality for the SNP Optimizer continue to use it into production, but I have seen several companies that have tried. What they found was that the extra processing time for the optimizer was quite high.

Interestingly, even if there is no source of supply (that is, no PPM/PDS and no external procurement relationship), SNP still creates the stock transfer requisition, but creates it without a source of supply assigned to the stock transport requisition.

When using multi-source functionality, the choice of supply source can base upon the following criteria:

1. A priority on the product-specific transportation lane.

2. A quota arrangement on the product-specific transportation lane.

3. A cost on the transportation lane for product that is already produced and product that still must be produced.

The Multi-sourcing Requirement
In the perfect scenario, one location would have a higher cost to supply than a second location. However, when the primary sourcing location runs out of capacity, the optimizer, in theory, will then move to the secondary source of supply, without the planner having to do anything. The diagram on the following page can be used to help understand this:

Multi Source Supply Planning

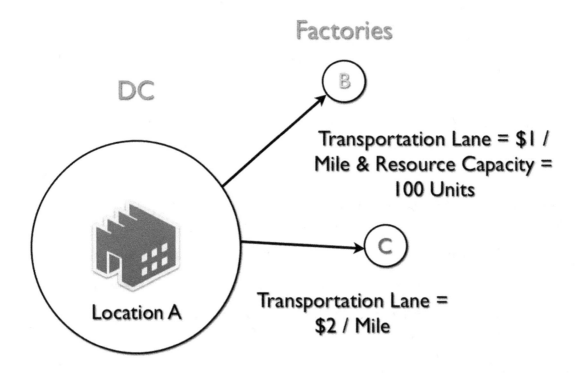

In this scenario, two producing locations have been set up as sources of supply for location A, which is a DC. If the requirements are within location B's capacity, location B fulfills the requirements from location A, because the transportation lane cost is only $1 per mile, versus $2 per mile as with location C. When the costs are set up in this way, nothing further needs to be done. The system will naturally source from location B. However, if in any one time period the requirements are higher than 100 units, location C will begin to serve as a source of supply to location A. If the resource that produces the product for location A goes down for maintenance, the resource has no capacity in location B, and C becomes the sole source of supply for this material to location A. Executive decision makers generally love that the system auto-adjusts, as shown in this hypothetical example, and foresee great cost savings from such a system. However, the reality of what occurs with multi-sourcing is quite a bit different, as explained in the following article:

http://www.scmfocus.com/sapplanning/2012/07/06/does-ctm-support-multi-sourcing/

The Reality of Multi-sourcing

The fact is, in SAP SNP, few companies actually make the jump to multi-sourcing. There are several reasons for this, and these reasons should be considered when selecting both a supply planning method and software.

1. SNP is a high-maintenance application. There are always many other issues to fix and other things to focus on before multi-sourcing can be reviewed. Often it can require years of fixing issues and focusing on other things until multi-sourcing can be reviewed.

2. Multi-sourcing greatly increases the run time of the optimizer.

3. Every client I have interviewed that started out with multi-sourcing turned on, eventually turned it off specifically because of the run-time.

4. Turning on multi-sourcing, in addition to getting resource constraints right and keeping them updated, is a heavy burden for even the largest companies. Both capabilities must be present for multi-sourcing to work. Therefore, while seeming relatively simple in concept, multi-sourcing is in fact one of the most evolved uses of cost optimization for supply planning.

Sources of Supply in PP/DS

This book is focused on sources of supply for SNP. However, it is worth noting that PP/DS uses the same approaches as SNP to determine sources of supply. For instance, its optimizer can also select from PPM/PDSs with different costs, can recognize quota arrangements, etc.

Time Validity of Source of Supply Controls

All master data objects that control the source of supply determination (which includes PPMs/PDSs and transportation lanes) have validity periods. These validity periods can be used to model the supply to reflect actual capacity at the time. Therefore, an alternate PPM/PDS, which can produce at some capacity, can be made available for only three months out of the year to reflect a higher capacity that is unavailable for the rest of the year. In the same way, validity periods can be used to make transportation lanes available—allowing transit to be planned between two locations, even though the connection between the two locations is not permanent. That is only one way to control the master data elements that control source of supply. For instance, transportation lanes can be blocked and unblocked, so that the transportation lanes do not actually have to be removed but can reside in the system and be activated when desired. Another way to do this, when the optimizer is used, is to change the costs of transportation lanes.

Conclusion

The standard sources of supply in APO are:

- Production from an internal location (production sources of supply are PPMs or PDSs)

- Stock transfer from an internal location

- Purchasing that is external to the supply network

All product locations are coded as either internally produced, externally procured, or both. Purchasing and stock transfer sources of supply are controlled in the transportation lane and a transportation line, like a PPM or PDS, can have either a priority, a quota arrangement, or a cost associated with it. Secondly, the way in which these elements that control sources of supply produce source of supply decisions is dependent upon the supply planning method used.

When there is more than one source and the sourcing is determined by the APO, the functionality is referred to as multi-sourcing. Multi-sourcing is the ability for a supply planning system to intelligently choose between alternate sources of supply. Multi-sourcing was explained in this chapter for both planning threads (network/MPS) as well as deployment, and for each method that is available in SNP for each thread.

In addition to presenting the official SAP stance on how each of these methods interacts with the master data objects (PPMs/PDSs and transportation lanes) to determine source of supply, I also included my observations from my project work, which should provide a good baseline to readers of where to be careful and where to be sure to test functionality before assuming that it works properly and can be put into service. The assumption that a company will be able to multi-source with a cost optimizer drives a decision to choose the cost optimization method over others. Generally speaking, this assumption is not practical, nor is it true in reality. In order to perform multi-sourcing with SAP SNP, a company must not only maintain the master data effectively for the multi-source option, but must also spend heavily on the servers to make the multi-sourcing model run effectively. In short, multi-sourcing is very expensive to do. If companies are not willing to support this very expensive solution, it makes little sense to head down this path. Right now, across the US, there are plans to turn on multi-sourcing in supply planning applications that may never work properly. This is one of the major areas of cost optimization that promises great things, but which companies are not able to implement successfully.

So what do companies do if the optimizer and the other methods in SNP are not reliable for multi-sourcing? Well, I have seen two options used on projects:

1. Update transportation lanes when the source of supply changes. This gets into the product-specific transportation lane, and blocking and unblocking means of transport.

2. A second way is to adjust the MOT with a table, which makes this change automatically; the planning group is then responsible for updating this table.

In addition to SNP, PP/DS determines sources of supply using the same master data objects (priorities, quota arrangements and costs); however, as this book is focused on setting up the supply network, we did not cover PP/DS in any detail.

CHAPTER 5

Managing Storage Locations with MRP Areas for Allocation and Global Available to Promise (GATP)

This chapter will describe a solution that has been used to protect allocations when sales orders are accepted. The solution was first developed in SAP ERP without APO, but APO can help support this solution. The first step to understanding this solution is to understand MRP areas in SAP ERP.

MRP Areas in SAP ERP

By setting up MRP Areas in SAP ERP, you will have more flexibility and control than simply using a plant. There are several uses of MRP areas, and because of this flexibility I, along with many experienced SAP consultants, believe SAP itself will often recommend setting up MRP areas, whether they are needed immediately or not. In this chapter I will discuss using the MRP area to represent a storage location. A storage location, as most people familiar with supply chain management in ERP know, is a stocking location within any type of physical location. Storage locations can be modeled down to the level of a SKU, or they can be aggregated. I will not spend much time discussing the warehouse management aspects of storage locations; instead I want to focus on the allocation functionality that storage location MRP Areas provide.

There are a variety of uses for MRP Areas; two of the major uses are listed below:

- **Plant MRP Area:** The plant MRP Area initially contains the plant, together with all its storage locations and stock with subcontractors. When you have defined MRP Areas for storage locations and for subcontractors and you have assigned the materials, the plant MRP Area is reduced by exactly this number of subcontractors and storage locations, as they are planned separately.

- **MRP Areas for Storage Locations:** You can define an MRP Area that consists of a particular storage location by creating an MRP Area and assigning the storage location to it. Material requirements for this storage location are then planned separately from the rest of the plant. You can also group several storage locations into one MRP area by creating an MRP Area and assigning the storage locations to it. These storage locations are then planned together. — **SAP Help**

This quotation shows that MRP Areas can represent a single storage location or multiple locations. In the following example, we will plan individual storage locations as individual MRP Areas.

MRP Area Storage Locations in APO

Let us review the quotation from SAP on the topic of MRP Area Storage Locations:

> *In SAP R/3, an MRP Area is an organizational unit within a plant for which you execute separate material requirements planning and inventory management. An MRP Area might consist of one or more storage locations (storage location MRP Area) or a subcontractor (subcontractor MRP Area). With MRP Areas, you can execute material requirements planning specifically for individual areas in a plant. For example, you are able to do this for individual production lines or for a store for spare parts. This enables you to stage materials for the individual areas in accordance with date and quantity.*

> *Processing using storage location MRP Areas is only possible for make-to-stock production. You only plan make-to-order or engineer-to-order production in the plant location.*

So MRP Area storage locations provide extra capabilities for the location. While there are many uses of MRP area storage locations, the requirement I will focus on here is the need to protect allocations per various demand segments (by customer or by customer group or by region, etc.).

MRP Areas in SAP ERP versus Locations in APO

SAP ERP and APO deal with the level below a location in different ways. In ERP, an MRP Area is a distinct entity, which is not a location. However, in APO many entities that are not geographic locations are represented as locations. A shipping point, which is simply a place in a plant where shipping takes place, is actually a location in APO. When a location is created in APO, it is necessary to define the location as a location type as shown in the screen shot below:

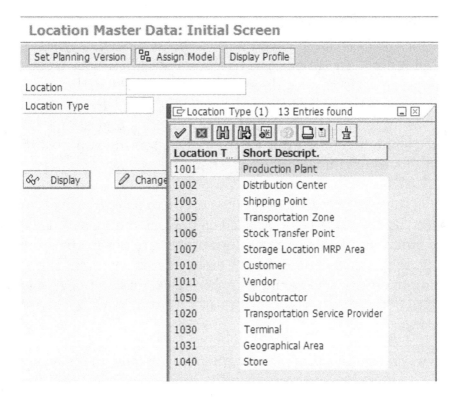

If locations come through the CIF from ERP to APO, then the type of geographic entity will cause the location to be created automatically as a particular location type. As you can see on the previous page, a storage location MRP area is a 1007 Location Type.

Background on the Requirement for Inventory Allocation in ERP/Execution

A major issue with many companies is how to allocate inventory for specific customers. However, for SAP clients that do not use GATP, the standard available-to-promise (ATP) functionality in the SAP Sales and Distribution (SD) module cannot utilize storage locations. That is, SAP SD cannot "see" below the plant/location in stock division. Thus, companies that need to allocate specific stock for groups of customers (for instance, geographic customers) must spend a lot of effort in order management to ensure that some sales orders do not consume stock reserved for other purposes.

The Lack of Persistence of the CTM-created Allocations

CTM is the supply planning method selected by companies when they want to create allocations—often for particular customers or customer types. While CTM can create "planning" allocations or GATP can have allocations created in different ways, an issue surfaces once the stock exists in SAP ERP because the allocations that are created in *CTM do not persist to the ERP system.* Therefore the allocations are planning allocations, not execution allocations. In fact, CTM allocations are only in effect after the network planning run is performed and before the deployment run is performed.

The benefit of the CTM network planning run when passed to deployment exists but is indirect, and tends to be overlooked on implementations. When deployment planning is run, those lower priority sales orders are not in the system to compete with the higher sales orders for the stock as it is deployed. However, this is disappointing to clients who would like the allocations and peggings to persist throughout all of the supply planning process. To read more about peggings, see the link below:

http://www.scmfocus.com/sapplanning/2009/05/06/pegging-in-scm/

Secondly, when the peggings that are created in CTM are passed back to SAP ERP, they can't be recognized or used. Therefore, the allocations and peggings are truly a logical connection, which is limited to the initial supply plan run created by CTM.

Furthermore, CTM is not used for the deployment planning run and neither the SNP Deployment Optimizer nor the SNP Deployment Heuristic can even see allocations or peggings that are created by CTM during the network/MPS planning run, so of course they can't deploy based upon these allocations or peggings either. In the vast majority of cases, the SNP Deployment Heuristic is used as the method for deployment after CTM creates the network supply plan or MPS.

CTM allocations are destroyed as soon as deployment is run in APO. This is a problem for companies that choose to use CTM, and after analyzing this issue and some spirited debate on this topic both with several clients and other APO resources, the consensus is that this is a basic flaw in the design of CTM. Therefore, while CTM is often described as an "allocation application," it may be more accurately described as "half of an allocation application." It is something that surprises many clients and reduces the value of CTM. However, storage locations are in fact *execution* allocations. One way of perpetuating the planning allocations that are created in CTM is to move the allocated quantities to specific storage locations that have been set up for different uses.

This is why it is important to use CTM along with GATP in order to support this design.

When Using GATP to Protect Allocations

However, unlike SD's available-to-promise (ATP) functionality, GATP in APO is designed to work with MRP Areas. The same product can be assigned to different storage locations, and each storage location can be provided with *a different rule in GATP.* Therefore, if for example a sales order comes in from a specific region, the rules in GATP can restrict the sales order to only pull stock from one specific storage location. There may be plenty of stock in other storage locations in the same plant, but if configured to do so, GATP will not allow the sales order to pull from them. In this way, stock is protected for some categories of sales orders (the example I show in the graphic is based upon destination region, but any category can be used).

The storage location is simply one way of providing an allocation to GATP. Another method is to create allocations with CTM in APO. Creating a queue on the supply side and the demand side, or possibly creating just a supply side queue or just a demand side queue generates CTM allocations. Furthermore, allocations can be directly created in GATP through several means.

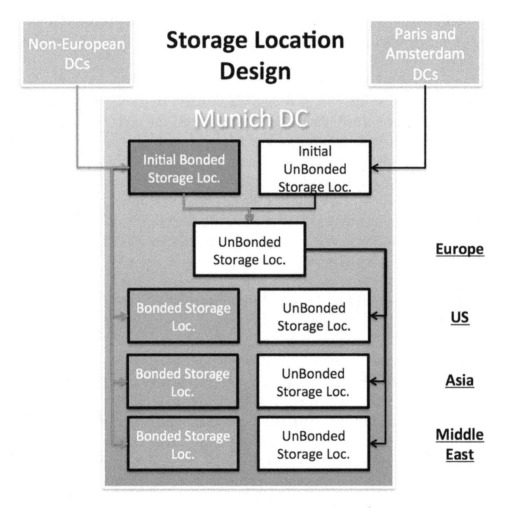

The logic for this configuration is really twofold. First, there is a basic division of prod-uct into bonded and un-bonded locations. A bonded location is not a separate location,

but is ordinarily a space in the overall warehouse in a caged area. Bonded stock can be released to either a bonded or un-bonded storage location (which I have called the "initial" storage location). In this example, the former happens when it is determined that the stock will be used for European orders. The latter occurs when the stock is allocated to a non-European region.

Each storage location can be made to be an MRP Area storage location. As soon as each storage location is an MRP Area, GATP cannot interoperate with this design. Without GATP, this is a manually intensive design with planners controlling the movement of stock between the different locations. However, when this design is connected to GATP, sales orders are routed to the correct storage location automatically.

The Implications of this Design for SNP

There are several implications of this design for various SAP modules; however, probably the biggest implication is for SNP.

1. There are now more product locations in the supply network to be managed. This is more an issue of organization and configuration overhead rather than an issue of processing time as is described in the third point below.

2. More product locations must now be added to the method profiles (SNP heuristic, SNP Optimizer, CTM), as well as more product-location combinations added to the selection profiles of the planning book. Within the planning book, what was once one location is now multiple locations which show the stock segmented into the storage locations.

3. A determination must be made as to how each product location must be planned. If CTM or the optimizer is used to plan most of the supply network, it makes little sense to use these complex methods to plan the storage location MRP Areas (as they are all at a single geographic location). This is yet another reason to use mixed methods in SNP. The main question to ask is whether there should be a push or a pull from the initial stocking location/ MRP Area to the child stocking locations/MRP Areas. As the intent is to create buckets of allocation, it makes the most sense to push from the initial bonded and un-bonded storage locations to the child bonded and un-bonded storage locations. This can be achieved by setting a target stock level (which

is activated by running the SNP heuristic), which allows each storage location—allocated to specific geographic regions—to be filled to a target. Of course, the presence of stock in each storage location is what GATP works off of when accepting sales orders and when decrementing them from the planned stock-on-hand at a particular storage location.

4. Ordinarily each product location must be assigned to a planning method. A planning method can also be applied to the entire network, but generally this is not how methods are implemented as there are a variety of methods and changes that are necessary.

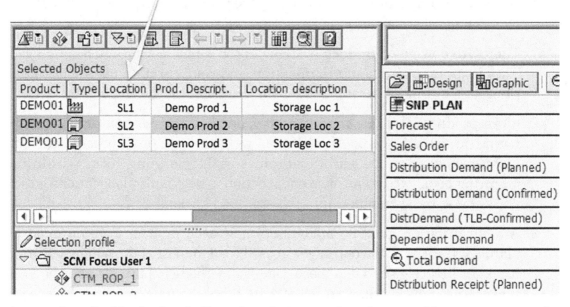

As was described in the first bullet point, the storage locations would appear as any other location or product location (which I have shown above) in the planning book.

Conclusion

MRP Areas provide extra capabilities to a plant in ECC. A major issue with many companies is how to allocate inventory for specific customers. However, there are limitations in ECC for doing this. One reason is the SAP Sales and Distribution module (SD) in ECC cannot "see" below the plant/location in stock division. Companies that I have seen protect stock in MRP Areas do so manually. Unlike SD's available-to-promise (ATP) functionality, GATP in APO is designed to work with MRP Areas. The same product can be assigned to different storage locations, and each storage location can be provided with *a different rule in GATP*. Therefore, if a sales order comes in from, say, one region, the rules in GATP can restrict the sales order to pull stock from one storage location only. There may be plenty of stock in other storage locations in the same plant, but if configured to do so, GATP will not allow the sales order to pull from it.

Using GATP along with Storage Location MRP Areas is an interesting approach to automating a process that requires a good deal of manual effort if GATP is not included in the design. The design described in this chapter requires that rules be set up in GATP that treat each storage location as an allocation. It also requires that the storage locations be properly planned in SNP. It's unnecessary to use a complex supply planning method to plan the initial or child storage locations, and a target stock level should help maintain the proportional stocks as desired. To see how this works in practice would require some prototyping, which I have not performed. Therefore, I cannot say exactly if setting a target stocking level would provide the intended result.

CHAPTER 6

Modeling Intercompany Transfers

An intercompany transfer is when one company buys product from "itself." While companies make a big deal about being global (and many certainly operate globally), when it comes to finance, a company must actually be incorporated in every country in which it operates, and must report to the tax authorities based upon its activities within a country. Thus, when a product (or service—but as this is planning we concern ourselves with products) is sent/sold between two different companies—say an automotive component from Toyota Japan to Toyota U.S.—an accounting transaction must generated to record that the product has been transferred. This transaction, which is dated and has a transfer price, moves the product from Toyota Japan's "books" to Toyota U.S.'s "books."

If you search for the term "intercompany transfer" in Google or on Amazon, you will find that most publications on the topic of intercompany transfer are on the topic of intercompany transfer *pricing.* I could not find a single book that covered the topic of intercompany transfer from the perspective of supply chain management. In fact, this short chapter on the topic is probably one of the longest treatments on intercompany transfer from the perspective of the supply chain in any book.

While accounting transactions are not particularly "relevant" for supply chain movements, they do have to be accounted for so that the supply network design can support the type of activities required on the accounting side. APO and ECC have a standard workflow for dealing with intercompany movements; however, the complexity comes into effect when the intercompany transfer involves more than two locations.

Intercompany Transfer Alternatives

There are two basic ways of handling intercompany transfers: a billing stock transport order STO and a standard STO. A standard STO is used between locations that are part of one company code. With a standard STO, no billing document is necessary because the STO is an internal movement.

A billing STO combines the document used for internal company movements with the invoicing aspect of a purchase order. This is shown in the graphic below:

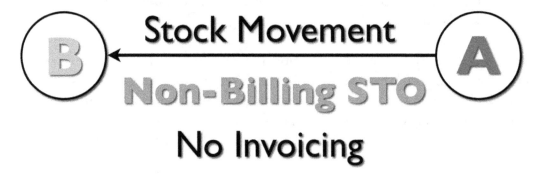

Normal Stock Transfer

A normal stock transfer transfers goods between two internal locations without any billing.

A billing STO simply performs the same movement, and then performs the inter-company transfer in ECC. This is shown in the graphic below:

Simple Inter-company Transfer

The first and most common method for intercompany transfer is covered by standard SAP functionality. It combines an internal movement with billing, hence the "billing-STO." Billing STOs work for straightforward intercompany transfers, but not complex transfers.

The billing STO is the most straightforward way of transitioning ownership between two company codes within one global company. However, it does not meet all of the requirements of intercompany transfer. For instance, some companies have multiple locations that interact with one another during an intercompany movement; while the billing relationship is between two locations, the goods are moving between different locations. Entities other than the receiving location can be involved in invoicing the sending location. In fact, there can be four or five locations (or possibly more, although I have never seen more than five location interactions). The standard billing STO will not meet the requirement because the billing ***is not applied to the location that is sending the product.*** This is a complexity that is missed by those that propose the non-billing STO for every intercompany transfer situation. (I know as I used to be one of those who proposed the non-billing STO at a company that had a more complex need than I first understood.)

Matching Purchase Order/Sales Order for Asymmetrical Intercompany Transfers

To understand this non-standard approach to intercompany transfer, we will begin by reviewing the standard purchasing goods transfer.

Standard Purchasing

Standard purchasing transfers goods from an external location to an internal location with billing. However, intercompany transfer combines features of both the internal stock transfers and purchasing.

Asynchronous Inter-company Transfer

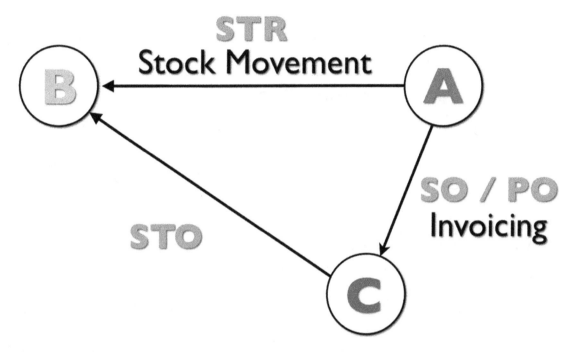

When the interaction between the locations is complex, and there are more than two locations, customization is required. Here the stock transfer goes between location B and A, but the invoices go between location A and C.

Custom Conversion Program

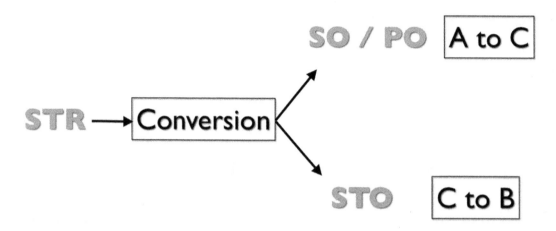

A custom program is required to take an STR, which in this case is created in APO, and convert it into several documents. One is the Sales Order and Purchase Order pair between location A and C, and the STO between location C and B.

Thus, while an STR is created in APO, once it is sent to ERP, that same transaction becomes a purchase order and sales order (which cancel each other out as they are for the same item or items and same quantities. The sales order and purchase order are simply two transactions moving within a company, or should I say two different company codes—a company buying and selling to itself). Let's review how the two different approaches work.

1. *Standard Intercompany Transfer:* When product flows from an intercompany location A to location B and the invoice flows from location B to location A, a billing STO is the standard and most direct way of managing the relationship between the locations. APO is unaware that the STO is billing or not billing. Billing is managed completely in the ERP system as APO does not deal with money. This approach is relatively easy to configure.

2. *Asymmetrical Intercompany Transfer:* When more than two locations are involved in the stock transfer relationship between two locations, the billing STO is not the way to set up this relationship, as it will place the invoice on the wrong location. In this case an STR is still created within APO between the sending and receiving locations. However, once this STR is sent to SAP ERP, the STR must be converted to matching purchase orders and sales orders. These items will move between additional locations beyond the two that are involved in the stock transfer.

A company involved in broad scale international stock movements will sometimes have different ICO models. Some of these models mean the creation of a paired purchase order and sales order from a stock transport requisition/order created in APO. Other movements may require no sales order, and in this case the STO is simply converted into a purchase order.

Controlling Transfer of Ownership in ICO Movement

In most cases the transfer of ownership will occur when the product is receipted into the receiving location. Although this is the standard workflow for ECC, it does not meet the requirements of all companies. Some companies want the ownership transfer to occur after the product has left the sending location but before it arrives at the destination location. I have found this to be true particularly of transfers with very long lead-times, such as ocean carriage. The graphic on the following page shows the standard transfer of ownership versus the custom alternative:

Intercompany Transfer Alternatives

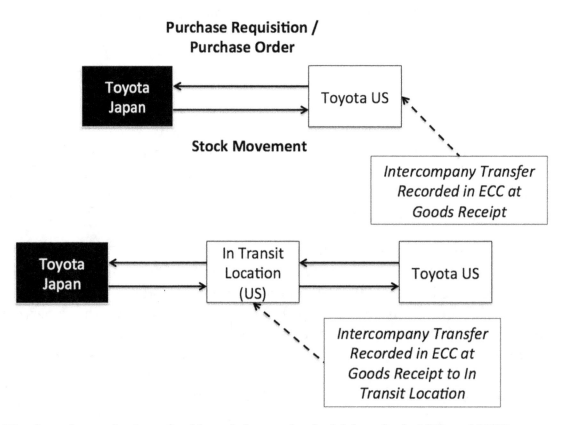

The first alternative is preferable as it is standard with how both APO and ECC operate. However, for different reasons some companies prefer the second alternative.

Because the transfer cannot be performed while the product is in-transit, an intermediate location, which is not an actual physical location but is a virtual location, is sometimes set up in order to perform the transfer. Some companies call this type of location an "in-transit" location. The location essentially has no purpose in APO because ownership transfer is entirely an ERP concern and is handled by the financial module in ERP. However, because locations (plants in

SAP ERP) that are created in ERP should also be represented in APO, the location is created in APO simply to provide continuity between the locations in SAP ERP and the locations in APO. The problem with doing this is that an in-transit location does not actually transfer stock between carriers. Instead, the location is simply where a change of ownership takes place. I have seen a design where the in-transit location is created in APO as a dummy or virtual location. While the design meets the needs of SAP ERP, the location is circumvented for APO, where a Means of Transport Transportation Lane is created from the first location to the third location so that the movement in APO does not involve the in-transit location. This is a high maintenance solution to the problem, although it meets the needs of both ownership transfer and the need by planning to only plan "real" locations. However, in SNP there is no good or simple solution for meeting this requirement.

Making a design decision like this is often a matter of trade-offs. Does the company prefer to accept more complexity in customization, or to have redundant locations? Whenever the supply network in ERP and APO do not match there are maintenance issues, which are inherent to the design.

Conclusion

Intercompany transfer is when one company buys product from "itself." Intercompany transfers are necessary because when a product is transferred between countries, its ownership changes from the company in one country to the company in another country. Intercompany transfers do not actually occur in APO because they are financial transactions in ECC, which is not visible to APO. However, APO must be set up to support the intercompany transfer in ECC, and that is the primary discussion point in this chapter. As this chapter demonstrated, intercompany transfers can either be simple and supported by standard SAP functionality or quite complicated. The complexity depends upon whether the invoicing is performed between the location that sends the product and the location that received the product and if the company can accept the transfer of ownership taking place during goods receipt at the receiving location.

CHAPTER 7

Capacity-constraining Vendors/Suppliers

A number of companies that I have worked with have requested capacity-constraining of suppliers. One can capacity-constrain internal production locations, but to determine overall feasibility it is necessary to capacity-constrain suppliers as well, particularly the largest suppliers. Because of changes to the business environment where manufacturing is increasingly outsourced, the requirement to either constrain or have visibility into suppliers has greatly increased in the past fifteen years.

There are several challenges to capacity-constraining a supplier production resource.

1. *The Technical Challenges of Modeling Supplier Capacity:* APO does allow for suppliers to be modeled, but as more of a workaround, which will be fully covered in this chapter.

2. *The Business Challenges of Modeling Supplier Capacity:* In the early stages of the project, project teams don't often consider how to get suppliers to provide continually-updated capacity information. When a process requires coordination between two companies, the results are uniformly worse than when the

process is managed internally by one company, even though collaboration has been talked up quite a bit. There are many different issues involved in collaboration, including the structure of the relationship between the two collaborating companies, the level of trust, and the incentives to collaborate. Authors of books and articles that have little interest in describing how things work in reality tend to gloss over these issues of collaboration. The fact is that few companies really know how to work collaboratively with other companies. Getting other companies to share their updated capacity information turns out to be a real challenge. The larger a percentage of business the customer company represents, the better the likelihood of getting compliance.

Technical Challenges of Modeling Supplier Capacity

Capacity-constraining suppliers can be both passive and active. Passive constraining is the most basic. Passive constraining tends to be used when the supplier is an "ordinary" supplier. Active constraining is more appropriate when the company is using contract manufacturing or the plant is essentially a "slave plant" to the company running the APO.

Over the last several decades, manufacturing has become intensively outsourced, and manufacturing is viewed less and less as a core competency. The most extreme form of outsourced manufacturing is contract manufacturing. Even companies that are very well known for manufacturing, like Toyota, actually do far less manufacturing than most people realize. The book, *Who Really Made Your Car?*, explains the high degree to which subcomponents are contract-manufactured in the automotive industry. This book, as well as several other sources, estimate that between twenty-five and thirty percent of the average automobile's value is actually produced by the OEM (Toyota, GM, etc.). The book, *Supply Chain Brutalization,* points out the following:

> *Automotive provides the volumes of consumer electronics, but contrary to the EMS ODM model of vertical integration, less than 25 percent of an automobile is manufactured by the maker. Components and subsystems, such as ignition systems, tail lights, interior liners, and power*

*seats are all subcontracted to third parties, rendering the car maker to
be a chassis manufacturer and systems integrator, so to speak.*

Who Really Made Your Car? further proposes that one of the major reasons for
Toyota's rise to prominence is not only its highly-touted internal manufacturing processes, but Toyota's ability to serve as a system integrator by developing
highly-collaborative relationships with the many contract manufacturers and
suppliers that make the majority of Toyota's automobiles (with Toyota primarily
performing the final assembly function). For some time at least, Toyota actually
took an interest in the success of their vendors—a very atypical perspective.

Contract manufacturing is explained in the following quote from *Beyond BOM
101: Next Generation Bills of Material Management* (Arena Solutions, 2011).

> *Since the late 1990s, outsourcing has become a way of life for electron-
> ics manufacturers. Most OEMs no longer consider manufacturing to
> be a core competency. Even in cases where some of this capability is
> retained in-house, there is an ongoing effort to evaluate more activi-
> ties that can be offloaded to a contract manufacturer (CM). These
> CMs, whose role in the electronics industry was previously limited to
> assembling printed circuit boards, have transformed themselves into
> large scale manufacturing powerhouses. Modern CMs provide their
> customers with a one-stop shop solution, providing excellence not only
> in manufacturing, but also in materials management, design and test
> services, order fulfillment and logistics.*

It is not easy to determine where a supplier ends and a contract manufacturer
begins, so I have included the following definition from Wikipedia to further
illuminate the subject:

> *In a contract manufacturing business model, the hiring firm approaches
> the contract manufacturer with a design or formula. The contract
> manufacturer will quote the parts based on processes, labor, tooling,
> and material costs. Typically, a hiring firm will request quotes from*

multiple CMs. After the bidding process is complete, the hiring firm will select a source, and then, for the agreed-upon price, the CM acts as the hiring firm's factory, producing and shipping units of the design on behalf of the hiring firm.

The amount of oversight of the contract manufacturing company by the customer company can vary from little oversight to a great deal of oversight. No simple relationship can be assumed. Some contract manufacturers are larger than the companies that buy from them and tend to do more of the planning and maintain more control. In those situations, a passive form of planning would fit the business requirement. However, there are also cases where the customer company wants a high degree of control over the slave plant, to the point of actually performing production scheduling, which can be performed quite effectively by SAP APO.

If a customer company wants to perform detailed scheduling of the slave plant, they would implement PP/DS or another production planning and scheduling tool, and essentially provide the run sequence to the slave plant. The slave plant can be given access to the PP/DS planning board, check it, and simply make the schedule determined by the customer company. However, this scenario is rare.

The more common scenario is for the customer company to perform either active or passive supply planning and initial production planning, and to allow the slave plant to perform its own production scheduling. Under this scenario, purchase requisitions are created between the internal location and the vendor location (in APO), and these purchase requisitions initiate planned orders at the vendor location. The easiest way for people with some SNP exposure to understand this relationship is to think of it as if the requisition (which in this case would be a stock transport requisition) were being sent between two internal locations. Everything is the same, including where the requisition appears (in the Distribution Receipt key figure in the planning book at the internal location, and the Distribution Demand key figure in the planning location at the vendor location).

Is there any value in going into the vendor planning book product locations if they are planned with a finite method like CTM or the optimizer? There can be value. While the requisitions or planned orders would not necessarily be altered in the vendor product locations, the planning book can still serve as a valuable reporting tool. For instance, one could select any aggregation of vendors and quickly see the planned orders and purchase requisitions per period. Creating a selection profile in the planning book for all product and vendor location combinations would enable this type of reporting. Of course, any subset of product or vendor location could also be viewed in a similar manner.

In APO there are two basic ways to model vendors/suppliers, one of which is the standard way. I discovered the second way by working on projects and it is not well-explained.

1. Modeling the Supplier Location as an Internal Location

2. Emulating Supplier Capacity with GATP

I explain these two methods of modeling vendors/suppliers in the following paragraphs:

The Standard Approach: Modeling the Vendor Supplier as an Internal Location

SAP does not allow R/3 to place resources into a supplier. Secondly, SAP does not allow PDSs to be placed in supplier locations in APO. However, the resources in supplier locations can be modeled if they are set up as internal locations in SNP, and if these internal locations use PPMs. (For example, instead of being set up as a location type 1001 Vendor, they would be set up as a location type 1001 Production Plant. See the following article on the different location types in APO:

http://www.scmfocus.com/sapplanning/2012/07/05/location-types-in-sap-apo/)[13]

What this means is that the PPMs (resources, routings, and BOMs) must be maintained in APO rather than as production versions in R/3 and CIFed over, as is normally the case. In fact, the resources, routings, and BOMs cannot exist

---

[13] This brings up other complexities as well. Instead of purchase requisitions being generated, APO will generate stock transport requisitions as the vendors are modeled as internal locations or distribution centers. However, they can be created as billing STRs.

in SAP ERP because SAP ERP only sees vendor locations as sources of supply, which is to contain this as production information, and not as a location.

Focus On  The Evolution of the PDS

In covering this topic, I am describing the current situation with regard to APO in version 7.1. I have heard from consultants who work for SAP that, in the future, PDSs will be able to be adjusted from within APO—something that cannot be done currently and is a significant disadvantage to PDSs. This is particularly true when using a prototype to determine where it might be beneficial to be able to quickly create master data to build models. If eventually PDSs can be created and changed in APO, then it will be possible to use PDSs to model suppliers rather than PPMs. It will not change the fact that work centers/resources and production versions cannot exist in supplier locations in SAP ERP, but will simply allow PDSs to be used instead of PPMs.

For companies that have decided to use PPMs rather than PDSs, the following article explains when to use each:

> http://www.scmfocus.com/sapplanning/2009/04/24/pds-vs-ppm-and-implications-for-bom-and-plm-management/

Companies that choose to use PPMs will experience less of a change than companies that choose to go with PDSs. Companies that use PPMs would designate each vendor location as simply another location that would use a PPM. Most likely, they would continue to manage true internal production locations with production versions in ERP, and then manage vendor location PPMs in APO. Companies that use PDSs will find this design to require more maintenance, because now they must maintain both PDSs for internal production locations and PPMs for vendor locations, meaning that those who use the system must become familiar with both objects.

For years SAP has been trying to get companies to move to PDSs, making the argument that the PDS provides better lifecycle capabilities (until it became clear that no one seems to use PDSs in this way). The current argument for PDSs is that they are supported for the long term, while PPMs are not. In general, SAP's arguments for using PDSs over PPMs have never been coherent, and a number of their early statements about the PDS turned out to not be true. However, SAP has settled on the argument that PDSs are supported more and allow companies to access more functionality than do PPMs. I have worked on a number of projects where the entire PDS versus PPM discussion has been a distraction. Until the PDS can be created and adjusted in APO rather than created in SAP ERP and brought over to APO, SAP has generated a permanent need for the PPM, even if it is not chosen as the main manufacturing master data object for the internal locations.

Common Modeling Approaches to Vendors/Suppliers
Production takes place in internal locations and in vendor/supplier locations. In most cases, product that is procured externally will be in vendors/suppliers that are not modeled as locations in SNP. When this is the case, the lead-time is taken from the Procurement tab of the Product Location Master.

In most cases, just a portion of the overall vendor database is modeled as locations. Doing so requires more effort to set up and manage, and is only beneficial for certain vendors, such as those with the largest volumes or with the most critical products. Secondly, there are several ways to model vendors, the most important distinction being whether the vendor is capacity-constrained. In cases where the vendor is not capacity-constrained (which could be because of the supply planning method used, or because of an active choice to not capacity-constrain the vendors), then the vendor location is used more for capacity visibility.

The options for capacity-constraining a vendor location are mostly the same as for an internal location, with fewer options for the technical objects that can represent the capacity.

http://www.scmfocus.com/sapplanning/2012/10/12/capacity-constraining-supplier-location-in-snp/

However, I have also come across large companies with few vendors, who did model every single vendor as a location. In general, this is feasible only for those companies with few vendors.

Technical Setup of the Solution in SNP

The technical setup for this solution starts at the resource. When internal locations are planned in APO, the BOM, routing and work center/resource is set up in ERP, and then brought into APO through the CIF to create either a PPM or a PDS (master data objects that combined the BOM, routing and work center/resource). ERP does not allow external locations to contain BOMs, routing and work centers/resources. However, APO does allow this. Secondly, between the PPM and PDS, only the PPM can be created within APO. Therefore, when one needs to set up resources in an external location, the PPM can be created in APO but without representing the resource at the vendor location in ERP. Purchase requisitions are converted to purchase orders between the internal location and the vendor location, and capacity management at the vendor location becomes an entirely APO-related affair. Essentially, ERP never sees this setup, and in fact does not need to.

Routes between the vendor locations and the internal customer company locations can be created automatically as transportation lanes in APO. These transportation lanes are created from the purchasing information record in ERP. While it is not mandatory that all vendor locations be connected to internal locations with a transportation lane, this option does have some advantages with respect to consistency. However, transportation lanes do require more maintenance than the second option, which is not modeling a location, but using a planned delivery time on the Product Location Master. APO can use either the transportation lane or the Planned Delivery Time field, which is on the Procurement tab of the Product Location Master to calculate the transportation lead-time.

Supplier/Vendor Locations

Vendors can be modeled, or not, as locations. Vendors are set up as locations when the company wants to do the following:

1. View supplier capacities.

2. Constrain the vendor production on the basis of constrained resources.

3. Use the transportation load builder to build loads from the vendor to the company's own internal locations.

Disadvantages of the "Standard Approach"

The problem with actually modeling supplier resources in a location, which is the standard approach, is that it creates a lot of overhead. Companies have enough problems keeping their own resources up to date. Secondly, the effort required to set up this design greatly limits the number of suppliers that can be modeled. However, it is not the only option for modeling supplier capacity.

Emulating Supplier Capacity with GATP

Supplier capacity can be emulated with GATP through the use of allocations. Allocations stop a sales order from being accepted or from being confirmed if it is over the allocation. Allocations are much easier to set up than all of the master data objects that must be configured for SNP and PP/DS, thus allowing more suppliers to be "modeled" in the planning application and making the overall supplier modeling process much more sustainable.

This issue of sustainability is quite important because most companies that I have seen attempt supplier capacity modeling with the "standard approach," fail to pull it off successfully. SAP APO does make the standard approach possible, and SAP will often write it up as a way to design the supplier modeling solution, leaving out how difficult the process is to accomplish. They also do nothing to make the master data objects in APO easier to maintain. In fact, SAP plans to extend the ability to model supplier resources to the PDS, increasing the alternatives for companies that implement SNP.

GATP has the following interesting characteristics:

1. CIF synchronizes the data between SAP ERP and GATP in near real time.

2. The ATP check is performed in ERP when GATP is not available.

3. GATP integrates closely with supply planning for the order fulfillment process and commits to a customer's orders based on the input information provided by the supply planning receipt elements.

4. Four workflows connect supply planning or SNP to GATP:
    a. (GATP Check) ATP quantity (developed from inventory or MPS).
    b. (GATP Check) Sourcing (based upon product/location substitution: –GATP checks procurement for itself in a way that is not part of the supply plan).
    c. (GATP Check) Allocations management.
    d. (GATP Check) Supply plan (daily/weekly MRP run).

However, the allocations we are thinking of creating are not connected to SNP. If we placed the resources and PPMs/PDSs into SNP, we would rely upon SNP to tell GATP what plan can be available. This design has GATP working off of allocations that are entered into the system and that serve as a proxy for the resources of the suppliers. This gets into the next topic, which is setting up allocations in GATP and how they are assigned to the product-location combination.

http://www.scmfocus.com/sapplanning/2012/08/21/using-gatp-allocations-for-modeling-supplier-capacity/

Allocation creation in GATP is quite flexible. Using it to model supplier as well as subcontractor capacity requires less maintenance than when the capacity is modeled in SNP. Performing constraint-based planning with anything but a small number of suppliers requires a significant amount of overhead, making GATP an important alternative. In fact, even unconstrained, it is quite a bit of work to manage supplier constraints through the standard process of setting up suppliers as internal locations, modeling their production lines, and then updating the production line capacity. More details on the GATP design to model supplier capacity are provided in the article below:

http://www.scmfocus.com/sapplanning/2012/08/21/using-gatp-allocations-for-modeling-supplier-capacity/

While the SNP-based design essentially takes the hard way, the GATP approach to supplier capacity constraints is the easier way. Instead of applying updated capacity information to the resource in the PPM, it is applied directly to the allocation in GATP. Of course the allocations must also be produced. This can be accomplished by setting target stock levels at the internal locations, which receive stock purchase orders to the supplier that match the allocation quantities. These target stock levels would be set in a way consistent with the desired allocations. The allocations functionality in GATP is very flexible; allocations can be applied to a combination of a customer and product, for just a product, for a product group, etc. The allocation, in effect, becomes a proxy for the production constraint. In fact, GATP has so many ways of setting up allocations and being configured, that the biggest challenge with GATP is simply making a decision of how to set it up.

The GATP approach is both feasible and lower maintenance when compared to the traditional SNP-centric approach to "modeling" supplier constraints. However, for whatever reason, this approach is not recommended frequently to clients. It may be that constraint-based planning is the province of SNP and PP/DS. It may also be that the allocation approach differentiates the management of the internally planned production locations differently from supplier production locations. However, this should not be a concern. It had occurred to me that one could manage all locations—both internal production locations and external production locations—in this same way. But, I am not familiar with a reference account for this design.

Technical Collaboration Challenges with SAP

In this chapter, I have spent a good deal of time describing the pros and cons of various modeling decisions that must be made when modeling supplier resources; however, these are not the only technical challenges. While it is often listed under business challenges, one of the issues affecting the propensity of companies to collaborate is whether or not the technology enables collaboration. Books on SAP do not address this topic, nor have I read any books on collaboration that have addressed it. In my view, this is because it is a universal requirement that authors talk up the technology rather than provide a more objective explanation. However, the truth is that SAP generally, as well as SAP APO, is rated poorly for collaboration. In my book, *The Bill of Materials in Excel, ERP, Planning and PLM/BMMS Software*, I write in great length about a company called Arena Solutions, which sets the gold standard in terms of collaboration. The difference between Arena Solutions and what SAP offers is a yawning chasm. SAP does have collaborative products, such as the widely discussed but very lightly implemented SAP SNC (Supplier Network Collaboration), but none of their products really enable collaboration. SAP continues to promote collaboration, but many of its collaboration products such as Netweaver and HANA simply don't exist in any meaningful way.

http://www.scmfocus.com/sapprojectmanagement/2010/07/netweaver-does-not-exist/

http://www.scmfocus.com/scmbusinessintelligence/2011/11/is-gartner-now-distributing-sap-press-releases-as-analysis/

SAP's problems with collaboration are multi-dimensional and are described in the article below:

http://www.scmfocus.com/supplychaincollaboration/2010/06/flaws-in-saps-collaboration-technology/

There is a second problem with obtaining resource information from suppliers. Due to SAP's limited security model, it's difficult to provide suppliers with access to update the resource values directly in the system. Arena Solutions can do this easily—not with resources, as they don't make planning products, but with their specialty, the bill of materials.

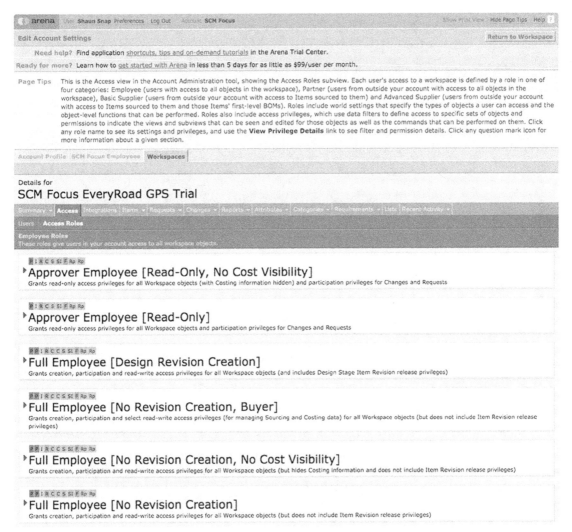

The colored boxes above the role (or the black and white boxes, if you are reading the printed edition of this book) define many different types of access. Because a fine level of control is allowed, access rights can be distributed broadly, both inside and outside the company that runs the application. This type of security, along with having a well-designed and easy-to-use user interface and with being natively web-based (SNC has several HTML "punch out" screens, but most of the application is built on the internally-oriented SAPGUI), means that the application is capable of truly supporting collaboration.

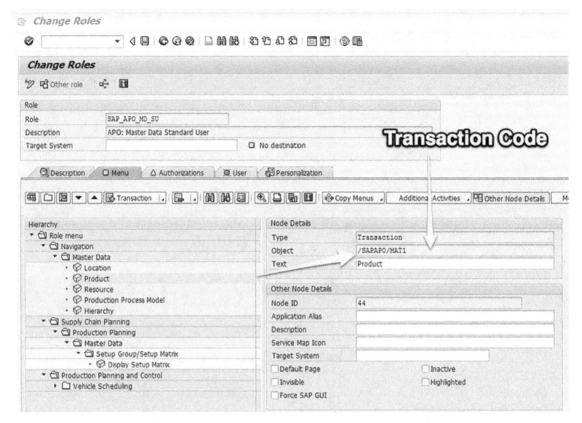

The problem with SAP's authorization model is that it is based upon the transaction. Authorization objects are below the transaction, but they take more effort to configure and to maintain. Because new users are being added perpetually and adjustments must be made in the security setting for other factors, a good security design must allow for changes to be made easily. This is covered in the following article:

http://www.scmfocus.com/sapplanning/2012/12/13/security-authorizations-in-sap-apo/

The Business Challenges of Modeling Supplier Capacity

Projects that model supplier capacity share similar business challenges to all other forms of supply chain collaboration (and perhaps non supply chain collaboration as well, but as I don't work outside of supply chain planning, I can't say for sure). Many factors reduce the effectiveness of collaboration.

The book, *Supply Chain Brutalization,* by Walt Grishcuk is quite illuminating about many aspects of contract manufacturing, including how badly contract manufacturers are often treated by original equipment manufacturers (OEMs). First, it's important to consider how little CMs are paid. For instance, while Foxconn employs around half as many people as Walmart, their revenue is only fifteen percent of Walmart's revenue (as the Chinese currency is undervalued by roughly one half, on the basis of purchasing power parity, we might adjust this value up to 30 percent). Foxconn profit margin is roughly 3.7 percent, which is quite common in the contract manufacturing industry. There are many reasons as to why the profit margins are so low for CMs. Some of the profit is simply stripped out by OEMs, both through the contract negotiations and also by forcing the CMs to hold inventory without compensation when things are slow. As pointed out by Walt Grishuck, poor planning by the OEM can be pushed on to the CM. In fact, many OEMs use "lean" terminology in order to force suppliers to do things that are bad for the supplier but good for the OEM, as is brought up in the book, *Supply Chain Brutalization.*

> *There are several ways to achieve cost reductions. Earlier we mentioned the brutal ways in which SCI was tormented each quarter by Racal. Is it safe to say that they would not have achieved the price points if they weren't so tenacious? Yes. But, look at the total costs, including the loss of revenue, which also occurred due to poor execution of the team and the resultant lack of desire of the CM to service them (business at a loss). Then add the costs associated with moving their manufacturing to a new supplier.*

> *We now operate in a brutal environment where the OEMs look for the company that can produce the products that will pass inspection for the lowest cost. This results in the sourcing of manufacturing in places that have the lowest labor rates, sometimes less than humane treatment to its workforce, and the least amount of regulations on how the enterprise operates in its community or affects its environment.*

It's very difficult to see how "collaboration" can occur in such an environment. However, mistreating suppliers and then asking them to enter information in a collaboration system happens all too often. Poor treatment of suppliers not only reduces collaboration, but also reduces the incentive for sophisticated supply chain planning. It's interesting that so few books discuss this topic, but Walt's is one that does, and does so in a very honest fashion. No doubt it won't sell as well as books that promote "twenty-first century-based collaboration," because most readers prefer fantasy over reality and a simple storyline that only discusses the upside. This is the approach of many consulting companies as well. They simply sell the potential of collaboration. That is the best approach to achieving maximum sales.

Conclusion

Capacity-constraining suppliers is a very popular topic in companies, and is a growing requirement as companies outsource more of their manufacturing, and manufacturing is seen decreasingly as a core area of the business. However, there are very significant barriers to modeling supplier capacity, not the least of which is that outsourced manufacturers are different organizations and are often quite geographically remote from the company procuring the manufactured items. While the latest article from the *Harvard Business Review* or white paper from Booz Allen Hamilton may be quite positive about the potential for modeling supplier capacity, the results are uniformly worse for supplier capacity modeling than when one company manages the process internally.

Capacity-constraining suppliers can be both passive and active. Passive constraining is the most basic and tends to be used when the supplier is an "ordinary" supplier. There are two basic ways in APO to model vendors/suppliers. One is the standard way, and the second is a way that is not generally explained but that I discovered while working on projects.

1. Modeling the Supplier Location as an Internal Location

2. Emulating Supplier Capacity with GATP

When modeling suppliers in APO, there are some important distinctions to be aware of regarding whether to use PPMs or PDSs to model the supplier, and how supplier locations are modeled in APO versus SAP ERP. As noted above, the second approach to modeling supplier capacity in APO is with the use of allocations in GATP. Allocations stop a sales order from being accepted, or from being confirmed if it is over the allocation. Allocations are much easier to set up than all of the master data objects that must be configured for SNP and PP/DS when using the first option above—the "standard approach." This issue of sustainability is quite important because most companies that I have seen attempting supplier capacity modeling with the standard approach fail to pull it off successfully.

The security and authorization model in SAP make it less likely that collaboration will occur, and therefore less likely that the resource information can be brought into SAP without an unreasonable amount of effort. When companies go down the path of modeling supplier capacity, they should be aware of these inherent collaborative limitations. These limitations are related to SAP's fundamental design and need to approve the appropriate amount of resources to overcome these issues. A company called Arena Solutions sets the standards in terms of security, and truly enables collaboration by making it easy to manage and change security functionality.

CHAPTER 8

Conclusion

This book started off by explaining how locations are set up and how they work in APO. The Location Master aggregates a series of fields to different tabs by category. Each location that is set up must be set up as a specific location type. Locations are generally brought over from ECC into APO from the CIF; however, there is still master data setup to be performed once the locations have been brought into APO, as some of the data for the locations is referred to as "APO-maintained data."

Some—although not all—locations in APO are connected to one another by transportation lanes. Transportation lanes control the flow of material through the supply network and determine the valid location-to-location combinations in the network. In APO, transportation lanes are complex, multi-dimensional master data objects. They also contain a large number of fields that provide a high degree of functionality, but which also result in a high-maintenance master data object.

SNP is a system that uses static lead-times. This is the way that supply planning systems, aside from multi-echelon applications, work. MEIO has the mathematics to calculate adjustable effective lead-times, which the system then uses to make more advanced decisions than are available to any other supply planning method. Lead times are one of the most important assumptions of a supply planning system; however, it can be surprising that the lead times—which are represented by the Transportation Duration field on the Means of Transport Transportation Lane in APO—are not more accurate (which is true in companies that use SAP as well as those that do not). Companies tend to spend little money and invest minimal amounts of time on determining and keeping lead times accurate. For whatever reason, forecast accuracy is of great interest, while the accuracy of lead times, which are just as important in determining the accuracy of the plan, is not.

A major component of what supply planning does is to determine sources of supply. The standard sources of supply in APO are either production from an internal location (production sources of supply are PPMs or PDSs), stock transfer from an internal location, and purchasing that is external to the supply network. All product locations are coded to indicate whether they are internally-produced, externally-procured, or both. In the master data objects, the settings which control source of supply interact with the supply planning method that is used in order to determine source of supply. When there is more than one source and the sourcing is determined by APO, the functionality is referred to as multi-sourcing. Multi-sourcing is the ability for a supply planning system to intelligently choose between alternate sources of supply.

Intercompany transfer is when one company buys product from "itself." When a product (or service—but as this is planning we will only be concerned with products) is sent or sold between two different companies, say an automotive component from Toyota Japan to Toyota US, an accounting transaction must created to record that the product has been transferred. Intercompany transfers can be either simple and supported by standard SAP functionality or quite complicated, depending upon whether the invoicing is performed between the location that sends the product and the location that received the product, and if the company can accept the transfer of ownership when the product is received at the receiving location.

Capacity-constraining suppliers is a very popular topic in companies, and is a growing requirement as companies outsource more of their manufacturing, and manufacturing is seen decreasingly as a core area of the business. However, there are very significant barriers to modeling supplier capacity, not the least of which is that outsourced manufacturers are different organizations and are often quite geographically remote from the company procuring the manufactured items. While the latest article from the *Harvard Business Review* or white paper from Booz Allen Hamilton may be quite positive about the potential for modeling supplier capacity, the results are uniformly worse for supplier capacity modeling than when one company manages the process internally. Capacity-constraining suppliers can be both passive and active. Passive constraining is the most basic and tends to be used when the supplier is an "ordinary" supplier. There are two basic ways in APO to model vendors/suppliers. One is the standard way, and the second is a way that is not generally explained but that I discovered while working on projects.

1. Modeling the Supplier Location as an Internal Location

2. Emulating Supplier Capacity with GATP

After the supply network has been set up, one of the best ways to take advantage of that work is to create a copy in a simulation version. Simulation versions duplicate the master data and the transaction data to create a snapshot in time. However, simulation versions do not affect the live version and are not connected to the ERP system. Therefore, they can be used to test anything, including the effect of changes to the supply network.

Setting up the supply network for SNP is a significant amount of work, even if just the basic location types are used. One of the most important factors to a successful SNP implementation is limiting the complexity of the supply network that is being set up. However, this factor is of course contrary to the reasons that companies choose APO/SNP (i.e., because of its highly varied and extensive functionality). However, it should be emphasized that decisions should be made with respect to how much of the SNP functionality can reasonably be activated and maintained in any one implementation.

The Supply Network and Simulation

At this point it is important to know that after a supply network has been configured, it can be copied to an inactive version (also called a simulation version). The inactive version is useful when the initial supply network is being set up, as different designs can be tested on the inactive version to see how they work. However, the inactive version can also be used at any point to test possible changes to the supply network. The process of testing changes is to make a copy of the planning version, make a change to a supply network element, perform a planning run, and then compare the output to the live version. Simulation versions provide flexibility because they are not connected to, nor do they send or receive information from, the ERP system, meaning that the simulation version can be changed radically and tested without having any effect on the live systems.

I put supply network changes into two categories. One is where the change is relatively minor and thus would be made in the live environment, such as changing the lead times on the transportation lanes. A larger change could mean adding several locations.

A simulation could be created to determine the effect of changes that are being considered strategically. However, while this is possible to do, I would consider it to be only theoretical. Realistically, it is so much work to make significant changes to APO's master data and to create new transaction data (the transaction data could not come from ECC as the simulation version is not connected to the ECC), that it is highly unlikely a company would approve the time and expense to make the changes to a simulation version when the desired information could be obtained by using a spreadsheet to estimate the effect of new locations on things like inventory holding costs. However, if only a small number of transactions were required (for instance, simply to see how data flowed between the new locations, and for use in creating a prototype and to get feedback from planners), a simulation version could be used effectively for this purpose.

The topic of simulation has a subsite at SCM Focus.

http://www.scmfocus.com/supplychainsimulation/

References

Issues in capturing in-transit in SNP interactive planning book. Last
   modified May 20, 2010.
   http://scn.sap.com/thread/1691155.

ATP stock categories CS and CA/CN usage. Last modified Nov. 7, 2011.
   http://scn.sap.com/thread/2072908.

Source Determination in Supply Network Planning.
   http://help.sap.com/saphelp_scm70/helpdata/en/da/8df3128121304a8dc
   1eef961a6d3a8/content.htm?frameset=/en/0e/7fd6b2aafc9a45a90d5ae
   32cc50120/frameset.htm.

Source of Supply.
   http://help.sap.com/saphelp_scm70/helpdata/en/0e/7fd6b2aafc9a45a90
   d5ae32cc50120/content.htm?frameset=/en/0e/7fd6b2aafc9a45a90d5ae
   32cc50120/frameset.htm.

Source of Determination in PP/DS.
   http://help.sap.com/saphelp_scm70/helpdata/en/29/eb0d3dbd82fe2fe
   10000000a114084/content.htm?frameset=/en/0e/7fd6b2aafc9a45a90d
   5ae32cc50120/frameset.htm.

Integration of Storage Location MRP Areas.
   http://help.sap.com/saphelp_scm50/helpdata/en/9c/c98251178511d5b3f
   50050dadf0791/content.htm.

Stock Transport Order with Delivery and Billing Document/Invoice.
http://help.sap.com/saphelp_470/helpdata/en/4d/2b911d43ad11d189410000e829f
bbd/content.htm.

Integration of Storage Location MRP Areas.
http://help.sap.com/saphelp_scm50/helpdata/en/9c/c98251178511d5b3f50050
dadf0791/frameset.htm.

Dickersbach, J.T. *Supply Chain Management with SAP APO(TM): Structures,
Modeling Approaches and Implementation of SAP*, 3rd ed. Berlin, Germany:
Springer, 2009.

MRP Area.
http://help.sap.com/saphelp_45b/helpdata/en/c4/106956ae8a11d1a6720000e83235
d4/content.htm.

Stock Transport Order with Delivery and Billing Document/Invoice.
http://help.sap.com/saphelp_470/helpdata/en/4d/2b911d43ad11d189410000e829f
bbd/frameset.htm.

*Stock Transport Order with Delivery and Billing Document/Invoice
(Cross-Company-Code).*
http://help.sap.com/saphelp_erp60_sp/helpdata/en/4d/2b911d43ad11d189410000e8
29fbbd/content.htm.

Automatic Cost Generation.
http://help.sap.com/saphelp_em70/helpdata/en/d6/f6d9414b619c39e10000000
a155106/content.htm.

APO Location Priority.
http://help.sap.com/saphelp_em70/helpdata/en/f2/d6253b20cb4040e10000000
a11402f/content.htm.

Deployment Optimization.
http://help.sap.com/saphelp_em70/helpdata/en/5a/32f73e0f303d67e10000000
a114084/content.htm.

Source Determination in Supply Network Planning.
http://help.sap.com/saphelp_scm50/helpdata/en/da/8df3128121304a8dc1eef961a6d
3a8/content.htm.

Transportation Zones in Vehicle Scheduling.
http://help.sap.com/saphelp_apo/helpdata/en/fd/7ec84e1dd411d5b3be0050045571
f7/content.htm.

Links in the Book

Chapter 1

http://www.scmfocus.com/writing-rules/

http://www.scmfocus.com/

http://www.scmfocus.com/supplyplanning/

Chapter 2

http://www.scmfocus.com/sapplanning/2012/10/15/understanding-the-flow-of-strs-and-prs-through-apo-with-a-custom-deployment-solution/

http://www.scmfocus.com/sapplanning/2011/10/12/snp-optimizer-sub-problem-division-and-decomposition/

http://www.scmfocus.com/sapplanning/tag/deployment/

http://www.scmfocus.com/sapplanning/2012/07/27/the-connection-between-boms-routings-work-centers-in-erp-and-ppms-pdss-in-apo/

http://www.scmfocus.com/productionplanningandscheduling/2013/04/22/multi-plant-planning-definition/

http://www.scmfocus.com/sapplanning/2009/04/10/scm-location-types/

http://www.scmfocus.com/sapplanning/2012/07/05/location-types-in-sap-apo/

http://www.scmfocus.com/sapplanning/2012/10/12/capacity-constraining-supplier-location-in-snp/

Chapter 3

http://www.scmfocus.com/supplyplanning/2011/10/02/commonly-used-and-unused-constraints-for-supply-planning/

http://www.scmfocus.com/sapplanning/category/spp/

http://www.scmfocus.com/supplyplanning/2011/07/09/what-is-your-supply-planning-optimizer-optimizing/

http://www.scmfocus.com/supplyplanning/2011/09/23/transportation-lane-settings/

http://www.scmfocus.com/supplyplanning/2011/07/14/the-false-assumption-of-multi-sourcing-in-cost-optimization/

http://www.scmfocus.com/inventoryoptimizationmultiechelon/2011/10/redeployment/

http://www.scmfocus.com/sapplanning/2012/12/14/representing-a-partial-supply-network-in-apo-versus-sap-erp-and-stos/

Chapter 4

http://www.scmfocus.com/sapplanning/2009/05/05/source-of-supply-in-scm/

http://www.scmfocus.com/supplyplanning/2011/10/02/the-four-factors-that-make-up-the-master-production-schedule/

http://www.scmfocus.com/inventoryoptimizationmultiechelon/2011/10/redeployment/

http://www.scmfocus.com/supplyplanning/2012/01/03/the-problem-with-cost-optimization/

http://www.scmfocus.com/sapplanning/2011/07/14/attempting-fair-share-distribution-with-the-cost-optimizer/

http://www.scmfocus.com/sapplanning/2013/02/01/parallel-processing-for-the-snp-cost-optimizer/

http://www.scmfocus.com/supplyplanning/2012/01/03/the-problem-with-cost-optimization/

http://www.scmfocus.com/sapplanning/2008/10/11/snp-deployment-and-fair-share/

http://www.scmfocus.com/sapplanning/2013/02/19/discrete-optimization-horizon/

http://www.scmfocus.com/inventoryoptimizationmultiechelon/2011/05/how-costs-are-really-set-in-cost-optimization-implementations/

http://www.scmfocus.com/sapplanning/2012/07/06/does-ctm-support-multi-sourcing/

Chapter 5

http://www.scmfocus.com/sapplanning/2009/05/06/pegging-in-scm/

Chapter 7

http://www.scmfocus.com/sapplanning/2012/07/05/location-types-in-sap-apo/

http://www.scmfocus.com/sapplanning/2009/04/24/pds-vs-ppm-and-implications-for-bom-and-plm-management/

http://www.scmfocus.com/sapplanning/2012/10/12/capacity-constraining-supplier-location-in-snp/

http://www.scmfocus.com/sapplanning/2012/08/21/using-gatp-allocations-for-modeling-supplier-capacity/

http://www.scmfocus.com/sapplanning/2012/08/21/using-gatp-allocations-for-modeling-supplier-capacity/

http://www.scmfocus.com/sapprojectmanagement/2010/07/netweaver-does-not-exist/

http://www.scmfocus.com/scmbusinessintelligence/2011/11/is-gartner-now-distributing-sap-press-releases-as-analysis/

http://www.scmfocus.com/supplychaincollaboration/2010/06/flaws-in-saps-collaboration-technology/

http://www.scmfocus.com/sapplanning/2012/12/13/security-authorizations-in-sap-apo/

Vendor Acknowledgements and Profiles

Below are brief profiles of each vendor for which I included screen shots in this book:

Profiles:

SAP

SAP does not need much of an introduction. They are the largest vendor of enterprise software applications for supply chain management. SAP has multiple products that are showcased in this book, including SAP ERP and SAP SCM/APO SNP and SAP SCM/APO SPP.

www.sap.com

Barloworld

Barloworld has three hundred and fifty customers for its Supply Chain Planning and network planning tools, covering such industries as automotive, industrial, retail, wholesale and distribution. The Supply Chain Planning product set offers a focused Supply Chain Planning footprint.

www.barloworld.com

Demand Works

Demand Works is a best-of-breed demand and supply planning vendor that emphasizes flexible and easy-to-configure solutions. This book only focuses on the supply planning functionality within their Smoothie product, which includes MRP and DRP.

www.demandworks.com

Author Profile

Shaun Snapp is the Founder and Editor of SCM Focus. SCM Focus is one of the largest independent supply chain software analysis and educational sites on the Internet.

After working at several of the largest consulting companies and at i2 Technologies, he became an independent consultant and later started SCM Focus. He maintains a strong interest in comparative software design, and works both in SAP APO, as well as with a variety of best-of-breed supply chain planning vendors. His ongoing relationships with these vendors keep him on the cutting edge of emerging technology.

Primary Sources of Information and Writing Topics

Shaun writes about topics with which he has first-hand experience. These topics range from recovering problematic implementations, to system configuration, to socializing complex software and supply chain concepts in the areas of demand planning, supply planning and production planning.

More broadly, he writes on topics supportive of these applications, which include master data parameter management, integration, analytics, simulation and bill of material management systems. He covers management aspects of enterprise software ranging from software policy to handling consulting partners on SAP projects.

Shaun writes from an implementer's perspective and as a result he focuses on how software is actually used in practice rather than its hypothetical or "pure release note capabilities." Unlike many authors in enterprise software who keep their distance from discussing the realities of software implementation, he writes both on the problems as well as the successes of his software use. This gives him a distinctive voice in the field.

Secondary Sources of Information
In addition to project experience, Shaun's interest in academic literature is a secondary source of information for his books and articles. Intrigued with the historical perspective of supply chain software, much of his writing is influenced by his readings and research into how different categories of supply chain software developed, evolved, and finally became broadly used over time.

Covering the Latest Software Developments
Shaun is focused on supply chain software selections and implementation improvement through writing and consulting, bringing companies some of the newest technologies and methods. Some of the software developments that Shaun showcases at SCM Focus and in books at SCM Focus Press have yet to reach widespread adoption.

Education
Shaun has an undergraduate degree in business from the University of Hawaii, a Masters of Science in Maritime Management from the Maine Maritime Academy and a Masters of Science in Business Logistics from Penn State University. He has taught both logistics and SAP software.

Software Certifications

Shaun has been trained and/or certified in products from i2 Technologies, Servigistics, ToolsGroup and SAP (SD, DP, SNP, SPP, EWM).

Contact

Shaun can be contacted at: shaunsnapp@scmfocus.com

Abbreviations

(SAP) APO – Advanced Planning and Optimizer

APS – Advanced Planning and Scheduling

BAPI – Business Application Programming Interface

(SAP) BW – Business Warehouse

BOM – Bill of Material

(SAP) CTM – Capable-to-Match

DC – Distribution Center

(SAP) DP – Demand Planner

(SAP) GATP – Global Available-to-Promise

RDC – Regional Distribution Center

DRP – Distribution Resource Planning

(SAP) ECC – Enterprise Core Component (Formerly R/3)

ERP – Enterprise Resource Planning

ICO – Intercompany Transfer

MASSD – Not an acronym, but the mass maintenance transaction in SAP APO.

(SAP) MDG – Master Data Governance

MDM – Master Data Management

MEIO – Inventory Optimization and Multi-echelon Planning

MPS – Master Production Schedule

MRP – Materials Requirements Planning

(SAP) PP/DS – Production Planning and Detailed Scheduling

RDC – Regional Distribution Center

ROLAP – Relational On Line Analytical Processing

SAPGUI – SAP Graphical User Interface

(SAP) SCE – Supply Chain Engineer

(SAP) SNP – Supply Network Planning

S&OP – Sales and Operations Planning

STO – Stock Transport Order

STR – Stock Transport Requisition

SYSID – System Identifier

TDS – Target Days' Supply

TSL – Target Stock Level (is also the acronym for "Target Service Level." Interestingly in MEIO software, the Target Stock Level is based upon the Target Service Level – leading to more acronym confusion. But in this book TSL is the Target Stock Level).

www.ingramcontent.com/pod-product-compliance
Lightning Source LLC
LaVergne TN
LVHW080059070326
832902LV00014B/2312